Spanish for Mental Health Professionals

D1603427

Spanish for Mental Health Professionals

A Step by Step Handbook

A Volume in the Paso a Paso Series
for Health-Care Professionals

Deborah E. Bender, PhD, MPH;
Christina A. Harlan, RN, MA;
Linda K. Ko, MPH;
and Irwin Stern, PhD

University of New Mexico Press | Albuquerque

Sponsored by the North Carolina AHEC with a grant from the Duke Endowment.

Other volumes in the Paso a Paso Series for Health-Care Professionals
Step by Step: Spanish for Health Professionals—A Handbook for Novice Learners
Spanish for Dental Professionals: A Step by Step Handbook

Designed by Melissa Tandysh

Contenido

Acknowledgments

We would like to acknowledge the North Carolina AHEC and the Duke Endowment for their support of this project through the Spanish and Culture Learning Initiative. We would like to thank Alicia Gonzalez, a psychiatric nurse specialist, for her insights and suggestions related to mental health and substance abuse.

We also want to thank the Latina immigrant women who shared their photographs and their memories of their migration transitions with us. May their needs and those of their families and neighbors be better met as a result of this collaboration.

Introduction

Latino immigrants who are coming to the United States in the current
wave of immigration come with the hope of a better life for themselves
and their children. At the same time, these immigrants usually arrive in
the United States having left some family members behind. The choices
are difficult. On arrival, new immigrants face not only the challenge of
new customs, new foods, and new ways of living, but also changes in
family structure and responsibility for decision making in the family.

Mental health concerns and care are difficult for Latino immigrants
for many reasons. The very idea of seeking care for "mental health
reasons" is difficult for most Latino immigrants. There are many
possible explanations. Many don't think of their change of moods or
preoccupations or bad dreams as a mental health "problem" apart
from their daily struggles to adapt. Some don't know that there is such a
resource. For others, to admit to having emotional problems is a point of
shame that may be akin to having failed family expectations of personal
strength. Immigration concerns may be yet another reason that some
immigrants would not seek mental health care.

The changes surrounding arrival and adaptation affect men and
women and children differently. Children are often the first to learn
English, thus becoming the cultural brokers for their parents. This is
awkward and often results in a reversal of traditional parent and child
roles within the family. Women find themselves lonesome for their
mothers and their sisters whom they were accustomed to relying on for
emotional support and advice, particularly with respect to parenting.
Men, too, may feel lonely if they came in advance of wives and children.
Or, they may feel overwhelmed by the tremendous responsibility of
supporting a family in the American economy. Yet men have fewer
opportunities to express emotional needs. These situations can be
precursors to problems—within the family or within the larger social
community.

One's culture plays an important role in the way one expresses—
or hears—emotional or mental health concerns. An individual's words
and behaviors need to be understood in the context of their culture.
The challenge of explaining an experience or a set of feelings across
cultures—and having them understood—is a challenge for both the
Latino immigrant and for professionals who seek to offer comfort
and support.

Why *Spanish for Mental Health Professionals?*

Perhaps you studied Spanish in high school or college a few years ago or traveled to a Spanish-speaking Caribbean island on vacation. You picked up a few Spanish phrases and enjoyed ordering your lunch in Spanish. But now you realize that there is more to learn than "*¡Quiero Taco Bell!*"

Perhaps you studied a language other than Spanish but would like to be able to talk and work with Spanish-speaking immigrants—adults and children—who come from Mexico, Central America, and other South American countries and have settled in your community.

Spanish for Mental Health Professionals may be just what you've been looking for. The handbook and its accompanying MP3 files have been developed with mental health professionals, including psychologists, social workers, psychiatric nurses, and others with helping roles in mind. This handbook begins with a home visit to a recent immigrant by a social worker. They discuss the young woman's dreams for a better life and some of the difficulties she has encountered since her arrival. The handbook also addresses feelings of sadness and depression, flashbacks and other symptoms of PTSD (posttraumatic stress disorder), the use of alcohol and drugs as a diversion, family conflict, and the role that community agencies can play in mediating the stresses associated with the migration transition.

The materials in the handbook are intended for novice learners who may want to polish Spanish not used for many years. They are also useful for beginning speakers who need a few well-worded phrases to establish trust with a patient while waiting for a fluent bilingual speaker to arrive. The handbook is organized in a series of *pasos*—steps—each designed to be a lesson or a chapter. Each paso presents commonly used verbs and other expressions useful in mental health settings. Further, in each paso, an aspect of Latino culture is presented. There are six pasos, suggesting that a group of learners—perhaps your entire clinic staff—could work through this material systematically during six consecutive weeks. Each paso presents six to eight exercises to engage you in learning, practicing, and speaking Spanish. At times, you'll notice that a phrase is included in both standard Spanish and colloquial Spanish—you'll notice your patients using both.

The downloadable MP3 files present dialogues that appear at the end of each paso. Each dialogue presents one or more health professionals interacting with a Latino client. The settings selected are those in which greetings and only a few additional sentences are necessary. The situations are ones that occur frequently . . . but they are not difficult to understand.

The dialogues are recorded in different Spanish-speaking voices.

The speakers are Americans who have reasonably good accents; one American, who plays the priest, speaks "lump-along" Spanish—yet he makes himself understood. Modeling the different voices provides the listener with an opportunity to hear Spanish spoken in the native rhythm, tone, and accent likely to be used by many clients yet to have as models American counterparts. At the same time, including the less fluent "lump-along" speaker provides some reassurance that even a simple attempt to speak Spanish with Latino clients communicates your interest and concern.

Links to each dialogue are provided in the appropriate part of the text, but all can be found here: http://www.unmpress.com/shell. php?Page=Spanish_for_Mental_Health_Professionals_Audio.

A Few Words on Communicative Language Learning

Communicative language learning places the emphasis on speaking and listening—on communicating. Grammar and language structures take a secondary place. One of the best ways to explain communicative language learning is to reflect on the ways that a child learns to speak a language. As two-year-olds, none of our parents gave us a definition of a verb or provided us with a list of infinitives to be conjugated. We began by using one or two words to communicate our wants. Then we progressed to the use of whole sentences, using simple constructions. Often, we used verbs in the present tense and added a word like "yesterday" or "tomorrow" to indicate time. We got our message across; our parents understood us. Somewhere during our schooling, we began to learn parts of speech and different ways of assembling language. Being able to label parts of speech gave us the ability to express more and more complex ideas, but it was not necessary for our communication.

I (Deborah) studied Spanish in college. I studied; I learned vocabulary and verb endings; I got reasonably good grades on tests. Then, several years later, I had the unexpected opportunity to work in La Paz, Bolivia, with a small nongovernmental health organization. On my arrival, I realized just how poor my speaking skills were! While I understood most conversations, when someone asked me a question I often found myself unable to respond—until too late! I knew what words to use, but I couldn't combine them—in a timely fashion—into a complete sentence.

I realized then that there had to be a different way to learn languages—a way that emphasized communication (speaking and listening), even if the conversation only lumped along, rather than putting primary emphasis on grammar. The story has a happy ending. Through my continued adventures in public health in Bolivia and other Andean countries, the patience of my colleagues, and many encounters with community women and children in health clinics, my spoken Spanish language skills have improved, allowing me to share the richness of Latino culture and language.

As a teen, I (Chris) lived in northern Maine where French was the second language—spoken only by people with French-Canadian backgrounds. I realized that it represented second-class status in our community. With that came an appreciation for sociolinguistics and an interest in learning other languages. I chose nursing as a career because I believed my nursing skills would allow me to travel, learn other languages, and immerse myself in other cultures. It worked! I was a Peace Corps volunteer in Brazil where I learned Portuguese. Later, I moved to Puerto Rico and worked as a home health nurse to improve my Spanish. Still later I married a man from Haiti and began learning Haitian Creole.

When I was in Puerto Rico, I was concerned that my patients would feel cheated to have a "gringa" nurse with barely adequate Spanish. But, because many of my patients had family in the United States, they wanted to help me polish my Spanish, knowing that I might soon, perhaps, help a family member there. My patients were able to "pay" me back for my nursing care with their support of my language learning. It's been an interesting road and one I am thankful to have had the opportunity to travel. I wish you well in your travels and exploration of Spanish!

I (Linda) learned Spanish while growing up in Paraguay, South America. I was born in South Korea, but immigrated to Paraguay as a child. I learned to speak Spanish by singing songs and playing with friends. My first Spanish lesson was from Lily, a girl who lived next door. She was about my age (I was seven) and since we could not talk to one another, she taught me a song. I did not understand what I was singing then. But later on, I realized that the song taught kids to relate time and things that they have to do. For instance, the song says, "when the watch marks seven, it is time to wake up and brush your teeth," and "when the watch marks eight, it is time to eat breakfast with a glass of milk," and so on. Because of friends like Lily, learning Spanish was always fun and never difficult or challenging.

My family immigrated to the United States when I started college. I minored in Spanish and my childhood Spanish changed to become more like the Spanish spoken by US immigrant families. I noticed that Spanish was taught in a more practical way here. For example, the second person plural was dropped. It made sense since "vosotros" is an old form of Spanish and is hardly spoken by Latinos living in North America. Also, teachers tried to incorporate "slang," "cultural phrases," and even "Spanglish" into their lessons. This was very interesting to me because teachers in Paraguay emphasized traditional Spanish from Spain and discouraged use of slang. However, I truly learned to value the US way of teaching while working closely with Latina women in Boston. These women were from several different Latin American countries and most had little formal education. If I had approached them with my original Paraguayan Spanish, they may have understood me, but would not have felt comfortable with me. This book teaches practical and useful techniques of the Spanish language and presents mental health in the context of Latino culture. I am glad to have participated in the development of this book and am positive that it will be an invaluable resource for those who work with Latinos in the United States.

I (Irwin) grew up in Brooklyn, New York, at the time of the first major immigration of Puerto Ricans to the mainland. I learned some Spanish and more about Puerto Rican life and culture from the kids on the street and on the little league teams. Although I understood a lot—more from context than from actual comprehension of specific words—it was only in the sixth grade of elementary school that my formal study of the language began. I pursued Spanish through high school and majored in Latin American Studies in college. I got to know lots of Central Americans, Cubans who had fled Castro's revolution, and other Latin Americans. I was continually amazed at the rich varieties of spoken Spanish that I found in my many visits to Latin American countries during college and graduate school.

In my career teaching Spanish and Portuguese, I have focused my language instruction technique on taking into account the needs of a wide variety of students to achieve their communicative objectives. In recent years, I have designed instructional materials to aid health professionals like yourselves who are anxious to be of service to the growing Latino population. With just a very few basic Spanish language structures and an ever-expanding vocabulary, as presented in this handbook, you will learn to communicate and comprehend enough Spanish to conduct an interview. Not only will you increase your own satisfaction, but your Latino clients will likely express their gratitude to you for your understanding of their situation and its cultural context.

Though immersion study may be difficult for you due to your personal and professional commitments, learning the phrases in this handbook and its accompanying audio files will improve your Spanish communication skills. Even short conversations with native speakers will increase your understanding of how the language works and will greatly improve your skills.

We encourage you to step your way through this handbook with your colleagues; it is designed to be a tool for group study. We suggest meeting each week for sixty to ninety minutes to practice dialogues and learn useful verbs, related structures, and expressions relevant to the setting in which you work. You should feel free to do more exercises on your own of course, but you may find the handbook most useful in the group-study setting.

How to Use This Handbook

The handbook is designed for use by learners who want to improve their ability to listen and speak to Latino clients regarding the clients' emotional or mental well-being. The handbook is well suited for groups of learners with similar interests and language skills. It is designed for use in a traditional classroom setting or in a health-care setting where a facilitator—perhaps a person in the agency who speaks relatively well and has had some experiences living or traveling in Latin America—could lead a group of learners. This same facilitator needs to be experienced and skilled in working with small groups. In all cases, the facilitator should be someone who brings enthusiasm, encouragement, and commitment to the task of helping others increase Spanish communicative skills.

The first activity, "Para la reunión del grupo," should be prepared before the group meets. Practicing the dialogue and reading the story will provide vocabulary and language structures as well as a particular cultural perspective that will enrich your shared meeting time. In class you will want to answer questions about the photograph and the story, establishing a connection between the language and the culture. Sections two and three, "Verbos útiles en el campo de salud mental" and "Palabras y expresiones nuevas" ought to be explained and practiced during the group's meeting. "Instrumento de evaluación," section four, has been included to provide a guided set of questions useful in assessing a particular condition. These assessment tools may be used as they are presented or combined with the dialogue. "Actividades para divertirse" and "En la comunidad" have been included to give learners opportunities to have fun while practicing their Spanish language learning during the week between formal group meetings. The "Diálogo" gives the learner more practice in talking about mental health with people one might meet in the community.

We recognize that a facilitator may want to "pick and choose" among the exercises and activities, so as to adapt the handbook to the particular needs of the learners. Indeed, we encourage the facilitator to be flexible and creative in adapting the materials to meet the needs and skill levels of the learners.

To the Facilitator

Welcome to *Spanish for Mental Health Professionals* and thank you for taking the initiative to help your colleagues in their fledgling efforts to learn enough Spanish to communicate with immigrant Latino patients coming to your agency for health care.

Your role as a *facilitator* (one distinct from that of *teacher*) is a very important one. Your responsibility is to bring enthusiasm to the group and to encourage as much spoken Spanish (or "Spanglish") as possible. Use the dialogues, the story, and the questions asked in "Para la reunión del grupo" as icebreakers or warm-ups for your learners. The most important part of your role as facilitator is to "get people talking." In the beginning, even short sentences may be a mixture of Spanish and English and pronunciation may be awkward. Reassure your learners that this is a typical step in language learning. Compliment individuals' attempts to speak Spanish and encourage them to "keep the beat" even if it means using an English word instead of a Spanish word.

Encouraging spoken communication is important. It is better not to focus on "correcting" Spanish pronunciation or grammar until the learner is ready for it. Often, students will correct their own mistakes and improve their pronunciation after hearing the questions and answers modeled by you or other more fluent speakers. Be ready to give out kudos whenever possible. No one flourishes in an environment in which the learner is reluctant to participate for fear of "making a mistake." Remember, your role is to create a comfortable, encouraging, nonthreatening learning environment—the only mistake is not trying a new phrase!

Students of all ages enjoy stickers as rewards! A small investment in stickers at a local teachers' supply store can bring great returns from your students. We like the following stickers from Trend: "Spanish Praiser" (T-46101) and "Spanish Praise Words" (T-47043), which are available at http://www.trendenterprises.com/catalog.cfm.

If the conversation flows beyond the guidelines of a particular activity, follow it. Something has grabbed the speaker's attention in a way that is important . . . this is an incentive to tell the story. A learner who speaks about an important concern or issue will find the words, in Spanish or English, to express herself. Momentarily, the learner may forget all inhibitions about speaking imperfect Spanish. *¡Bravo!* Build on the speaker's story, ask questions, and encourage others to do likewise. The guidelines for the particular activity are there when you are ready to come back to them.

To the Learner

As you begin your adventure into communicative Spanish, set aside time to meet once a week at lunch or earlier in the day before the clinic schedule gets too busy. Listen to the recommended dialogue or dialogues well in advance of your group's meeting. Do practice repeating the phrases in the dialogue. Then, after you are familiar with the dialogue, try saying the health professional's phrases even before you hear them in the audio file. With practice, you will notice that a mechanical repetition of words begins to give way to a more rhythmical pronunciation that is characteristic of Spanish. With time, your ear will also begin to detect differences in pronunciation that are characteristic of different nations and regions in Latin America.

Between meetings, speak Spanish as often as you can. Set aside thirty minutes of each day to do something in Spanish. Visit a Latino-owned grocery store. Attend the Spanish language service at a church in your community. Go to dinner at a Mexican restaurant, and insist on ordering in Spanish. Watch a Spanish language program on television or rent a Spanish language video. Read—even a paragraph—in a Spanish language newspaper. You'll be surprised and pleased at the new words you add to your vocabulary. As you speak, try to express the idea in a complete sentence. Reach for a familiar English word if you don't know the equivalent Spanish word. It will probably work! But keep the rhythm of the language. You'll be surprised at how much of your meaning is embedded in the context of your conversation.

You may also want to begin to build a personal library of Spanish resources. A good dictionary and a book with lists of verb conjugations are essential learning tools. Watch for phrase books of interest. Begin to try to read short stories or novels. Reading children's books, often printed in English and Spanish, is a delightful way to learn more about different Latino cultures as well as to expand your working vocabulary. One word of advice—as one of the learners who participated in the Spanish and Culture Learning Immersion Workshop reminded her colleagues—"Use it, or lose it!"

The Organization of This Handbook

Spanish for Mental Health Professionals is divided into six separate pasos (steps). Each paso is a rich resource of activities from which you, the facilitator, may pick and choose for your particular group. In each paso, more material than you will likely use in one session is included so as to enable you to adapt your presentation to the interests and language skill level of your participants. You may also choose to use the handbook for an initial presentation and again, later, as a review and enrichment. This is often effective in demonstrating to novice learners just how much they have learned.

✦ We recommend that the first activity of each paso, "Para la reunión del grupo" (For the group meeting), be done before the group meets. This includes listening to the accompanying MP3 file, thinking about the photograph, and reading the story. The questions and answers about the photograph and the story are a good opening for the next workshop session. Encourage your group to imitate what they hear in the audio file until they are comfortable generating the phrases on their own. The dialogues appear at the end of each paso.

Latina immigrant women took most of the photographs presented in the handbook. These women were assistants in a study that sought to understand the role of social support on use of preventive health services during a migration transition. We asked the Latina photographers to take photographs of people or places that helped them access health-care services during their first years in the United States—as well as situations that posed a risk or challenge to their well-being. The story that follows each photograph tells of a personal family situation that is related to the paso's theme; they are based on personal stories told by the Latina immigrant women. Names used are fictitious.

✦ The next activity in each paso is "Charlas para empezar la reunión" (Conversations to start the meeting). These conversations help to ease the group back into the Spanish conversation lesson. Encourage participants to use their best available Spanish (or "Spanglish"). Each *charla* includes questions about the photo and the story.

✦ Each paso, in the section titled "Verbos útiles en el campo de salud mental" (Useful verbs in the field of mental health) introduces several verbs useful in mental health settings. Choosing verbs that are useful in talking with your patients and their families should make the task of learning verbs easier. Still, there is no substitute for memorization! Some people find that writing practical sentences that use each verb on flash cards is helpful. Why not try it?

✦ "Palabras y expresiones nuevas" (New words and expressions) is designed to expand your working vocabulary. The expressions are commonly used in greetings, conversations, and good-byes. Being able to use these expressions comfortably will help to establish a climate of trust.

✦ "Instrumento de evaluación" (Assessment tool) models a series of dialogues designed to help you assess a patient's condition or advise a person in your community about where to go for help. Please do adapt these dialogues to your own setting, adding and changing vocabulary, as they are helpful.

✦ "Durante la semana que viene" (During the coming week) offers additional activities oriented toward increasing your knowledge of the structural material presented in the paso as well as enhancing cultural awareness. It provides suggestions for you to actively expand on and activate your knowledge of the language and culture through a variety of tasks. Share your information or results with your colleagues in the following meeting.

✦ "Actividades para divertirse" (Activities for fun) are activities that are designed to reinforce workshop learning through puzzles and games that increase knowledge and understanding of Latino culture. Many group members will look forward to doing these activities because they are inviting and fun.

✦ "En la comunidad" (In the community) presents activities intended to entice participants to explore Latino culture within their community. Going to a Mexican restaurant, greeting the staff and ordering in Spanish, and viewing Spanish movies or reading children's books about immigration are examples. Consider talking about these experiences during a workshop session paso so that participants can link learning to living.

◆ "El diálogo" (Dialogue) is presented at the end of each paso. These dialogues are the same as the dialogues that are in the appropriate MP3 files. Remember: learners should familiarize themselves with this material before they come to each workshop session.

Be creative! Learners will surprise themselves with the ease with which they master new relevant phrases. Learners will also be surprised at how the language structures make sense with repeated use. Remember, an average learner must see something THREE times before recognizing it spontaneously and must hear something SEVEN times before "owning" it. If you are a native or seasoned speaker of Spanish, what seems redundant to you is critical to the learning process of novice learners.

¡Buena suerte! . . . Good luck!

Paso Uno

Charlando con la trabajadora social
Talking with the social worker

1. Para la reunión del grupo
For the group meeting

Antes de la reunión, escuche el diálogo, "Esperando una vida mejor como inmigrante" (http://unmpress.com/UserFiles/Audio/ Spanish_for_Mental_Health_Professionals/Paso1.mp3) y lea la historia sobre una visita a casa.

Before getting together, listen to the dialogue, "Hoping for a better life as an immigrant" (http://unmpress.com/UserFiles/Audio/ Spanish_for_Mental_Health_Professionals/Paso1.mp3) and read the story about a home visit.

1

1.A. Cultura latina en contexto
Latino culture in context

"Making a Home Visit"

We used to live really bad. We only had a table . . . Sometimes I didn't even have a diaper for my little boy.

—*María Guadalupe*

Carolyn is a mental health social worker who works at the local county Department of Health and Human Services. Her job is to assess barriers that Latina women face upon immigration to the United States and observe how those barriers affect their mental health. She uses a combination of methods, including personal interviews, home visits, books, and pictures about Latino life to better understand Latina women's background and the challenges they face making a new life in the United States.

Last week, she visited a young woman from Guatemala, María Guadalupe. Lupe, as she calls herself, told Carolyn that she had met her husband here in the United States. They were both from Guatemala, but they didn't know each other there. At first, it was very hard. "My husband was not making enough. He got paid twice a month, but it barely covered our living expenses," Lupe told Carolyn. Then, Lupe did not know how to drive a car, and buses were infrequent, so that made her adjustment to the new country even more difficult. "I couldn't drive so I needed Ramón to take me places. It's hard when you depend on your husband for everything," she added quietly.

Language was another factor that made their adjustment challenging. "I wanted to learn English, but I had to stay home and take care of my baby. It would have been nice if I did not have anything that held me back, to not have the worries of feeding the baby and everything."

Lupe acknowledged reluctantly that all of these factors eventually affected her emotionally. It seemed to be one thing after another. She added that her friends had experienced similar problems when they came to the United States. "My friend Lulu was stressed out, desperate, and depressed. She felt so depressed that she even had to go to a doctor!" Lupe feels that she is doing better now. But she still feels frustrated at times, living in the United States. She wonders if Carolyn can help her with some of these transitions.

1.B. Charlas para empezar la reunión
Conversations to start the meeting

▧ Mire la foto otra vez y piense en la historia que leyó. Esta foto es una de una serie tomada por algunas mujeres latinas fotógrafas de la comunidad. Esta foto la tomó el esposo de la mujer latina de la foto. Use su mejor español y su imaginación para describir lo que ve en la foto. Responda a las preguntas de abajo en español o inglés.

☺ *Look again at the photograph and think about the story you read. This photograph is one of a series taken by Latina community photographers. This photograph was taken by the husband of the young Latina woman in the picture. Use your best Spanish and your imagination to describe what you see in the photograph. A guide to Spanish pronunciation is available in the appendix.*
   Answer the questions below in Spanish or English.

a.   ¿Dónde están las personas en la foto? ¿Quiénes son las dos?
   Where are the people in the photograph? Who are the two people?

b.   ¿Cuál es la profesión de la mujer mayor?
   What is the profession of the older woman?

c.   En la historia, ¿de qué país es la mujer joven?
   In the story, from what country is the young woman?

d.   ¿De qué están hablando ellas?
   What are they talking about?

1.C. Practique el diálogo
Practice the dialogue

▧ En grupos de dos, repase el diálogo de este paso. Repítalo varias veces; note como su ritmo al hablar mejora con práctica.

☺ *In groups of two, review the dialogue for this paso. Repeat it several times, noticing how the rhythm improves with practice.*

2. Verbos útiles en el campo de salud mental
Useful verbs in the field of mental health

2.A. Los verbos "ser" y "estar"
The verbs for "to be"

Abajo, hay dos verbos en español que expresan "to be" en inglés. Ambos están conjugados en el tiempo presente.

Below are the two Spanish verbs used to express "to be" in English. Both are conjugated in the present tense.

Ser: *To be*		Estar: *To be*	
Yo soy	*I am*	Yo estoy	*I am*
Tú eres	*You are (informal)*	Tú estás	*You are (informal)*
Ud. es	*You are (formal)*	Ud. está	*You are (formal)*
Él/Ella es	*He/She is*	Él/Ella está	*He/She is*
Nosotros somos	*We are*	Nosotros estamos	*We are*
Uds. son	*You are (plural)*	Uds. están	*You are (plural)*
Ellos son	*They are*	Ellos están	*They are*

Note: In professional practice, you will use "usted" (or Ud.) almost exclusively, except if you are working with children. As you get to know your client better, you may choose to use "tú"; take your clues from the client.

■ *The verb "ser" is used to express professions, origin (birthplaces), time, and physical or personal characteristics of an individual.*

Professions:	Yo soy médico.	*I am a doctor.*
Birthplaces:	¿Es usted mexicana?	*Are you Mexican?*
Clock time:	¿Qué hora es?	*What time is it?*
Physical characteristics:	Ella es hermosa.	*She is beautiful.*

■ *The verb "estar" is used in connection with locations of things or people and with adjectives that describe states of being, such as emotions, feelings, or physical and mental health.*

Locations:	Ellos están en la clínica.	*They are in the clinic.*
Feelings:	Yo estoy triste.	*I am sad.*
Health:	Nosotros estamos enfermos.	*We are sick.*

Práctica A

Using the verbs for "to be," answer the following questions based on the story about Carolyn's visit to the home of María Guadalupe.

1. ¿Qué es la profesión de Carolina? _____

2. ¿Dónde están ellas? _____

3. ¿Qué cosas están en la mesa? _____

4. ¿De dónde es María Guadalupe?_____

5. ¿Cómo está la mujer latina aquí?_____

2.B. El verbo "tener"
The verb "to have"

Un tercer verbo que sus clientes o pacientes pueden usar al hablar acerca de sí mismos es "tener." Además de ser usado para expresar edad, sentimientos de calor o frío, y hambre, se usa "tener" para expresar sentimientos de culpabilidad, miedo, y vergüenza.

A third verb that clients or patients will use in talking about themselves is "tener." In addition to being used to express age, feelings of being hot or cold, and hunger, "tener" is also used to express feelings of guilt, fear, and embarrassment.

Tener: *To have*	
Yo tengo	*I have*
Tú tienes	*You have (informal)*
Ud. tiene	*You have (formal)*
Él/Ella tiene	*He/She has*
Nosotros tenemos	*We have*
Uds. tienen	*You have (plural)*
Ellos tienen	*They have*

Notice that "tener frío" and "tener calor" are used exclusively for people or animals. If you wish to say that an object is hot or cold, use "estar."

2.C. Usando el verbo "tener"
Using the verb "tener"

El verbo "tener" se usa en varias expresiones. Estas expresiones son usadas con mucha frecuencia para expresar los sentimientos. Algunos ejemplos más usados aparecen abajo.

The verb "tener" is used in many idiomatic expressions. These expressions are used by a person trying to express feelings or emotions. Some frequently used examples are given below.

tener . . . años	*to be . . . years old*	Ella tiene veintidós años.
tener calor	*to be hot*	Tengo fiebre; tengo calor.
tener frío	*to be cold*	Está enfermo; tiene frío.
tener hambre	*to be hungry*	Come poco; siempre tiene hambre.
tener sed	*to be thirsty*	No hay agua aquí; tengo sed.
tener miedo	*to be afraid of*	Tengo miedo en la noche.
tener vergüenza	*to be ashamed*	Tengo vergüenza de salir así.
tener celos	*to be jealous*	Ella tiene celos de su prima.
tener cuidado	*to be careful*	¡Ten cuidado en la calle!
tener la culpa	*to be guilty*	Tiene toda la culpa.
tener paciencia	*to be patient*	Tú no tienes mucha paciencia.
tener (mucha) prisa	*to be in a hurry*	Él tiene prisa. Va a llegar tarde.
tener suerte	*to be lucky*	Tenemos mucha suerte de estar aquí en los Estados Unidos.
tener fiebre	*to have a fever*	El chico tiene fiebre hoy.
tener dolor de cabeza	*to have a headache*	Tengo un dolor de cabeza.
tener un resfriado	*to have a cold*	Tu tienes un resfriado.

Práctica B

Describe the symptoms of the following people, using the correct form of the verb "to be" or "tener."

1. María Guadalupe . . . preocupada. _____

2. 95° grados; Luisa . . . calor. _____

3. Luisa . . . celos de su hermana. _____

4. Miguel . . . fiebre. _____

5. Pedro . . . hondureño. _____

6. Roberto . . . médico. _____

7. Ella . . . hambre. _____

8. El niño . . . resfriado. _____

9. Ana . . . en la clínica. _____

10. Los hombres . . . la culpa. _____

Práctica C

Choose a partner. Start a conversation about personal characteristics, professions, locations of people, or expressions of feelings. Ask your partner questions that require the use of one of the verbs "to be" or "to have." Reverse roles. Ask enough questions of each other so that the use of the correct verb begins to be automatic.

3. Palabras y expresiones nuevas
New words and expressions

3.A. Profesiones
Professions

Abajo, hay una lista de las profesiones más comunes de la salud mental. Busque el nombre de su profesión en español.

Below is a list of the most common titles for mental health professionals. Find the Spanish name for your profession.

Español	English
El doctor *(male)*/La doctora *(female)* El médico/La médica* *Note: "La doctora" is used more frequently than "médica."*	*The doctor*
El enfermero/La enfermera	*The nurse*
El recepcionista/La recepcionista	*The receptionist*
El psiquiatra/La psiquiatra	*The psychiatrist*
El psicólogo/La psicóloga	*The psychologist*
El terapeuta/La terapeuta El terapista/La terapista	*The therapist*
El trabajador social/La trabajadora social	*The social worker*
El consejero/La consejera	*The counselor*
El consejero pastoral	*The religious counselor*
La consejera pastoral	*i.e., minister, priest, or pastor*
El director del caso La directora del caso	*The case manager*
El técnico de salud mental La técnica de salud mental	*The mental heath technician*

3.B. Países
Countries

▓▓ Abajo, hay una lista de los países hispanoparlantes y las identidades nacionales de cada país.

☺ *Below is a list of Spanish-speaking countries and their nationalities.*

País/*Country*	Nacionalidad/*Nationality*
Los Estados Unidos	americano/a; estadounidense *(m./f.)*
México	mexicano/a
Guatemala	guatemalteco/a
Honduras	hondureño/a
El Salvador	salvadoreño/a
Nicaragua	nicaragüense *(m./f.)*
Costa Rica	costarricense *(m./f.)*
Panamá	panameño/a
Venezuela	venezolano/a
Colombia	colombiano/a
Ecuador	ecuatoriano/a
Perú	peruano/a
Bolivia	boliviano/a
Paraguay	paraguayo/a
Chile	chileno/a
Uruguay	uruguayo/a
Argentina	argentino/a
La República Dominicana	dominicano/a
Puerto Rico	puertorriqueño/a
Cuba	cubano/a

Práctica D

Below is a map of countries of Latin America. People from Latin America self-identify as being from a country more than an ethnic group. Learning some characteristics of national identity will help you to understand your clients' concerns. Choose a country and a profession to talk about. Go around the room, asking others to name their profession and tell you where they are from. Tell what you know about your country, in Spanish or English.

Práctica E

Describe—in English or Spanish—where each of the Spanish-speaking countries on the map is located (está ubicado) using the direction words north (norte), south (sur), east (este), or west (oeste). For example, "Paraguay está ubicado al sur de Bolivia" (Paraguay is located south of Bolivia).

4. Instrumento de evaluación: Conociendo a su paciente
Assessment tool: Meeting your patient

Español/*Spanish*	*English*/Inglés
◆ ¿Cómo se siente hoy?	◆ *How do you feel today?*
◆ ¿Cómo se sintió la semana pasada?	◆ *How did you feel last week?*
❯ Cansada.	❯ *Tired.*
❯ Triste.	❯ *Sad.*
◆ Yo soy la trabajadora social. *(female)*	◆ *I am the social worker.*
◆ Yo soy el psicólogo. *(male)*	◆ *I am the psychologist.*
❯ Mucho gusto. Encantado de conocerlo.	❯ *Pleased to meet you.*
❯ El gusto es mío.	❯ *The pleasure is mine.*
◆ Pase adelante por favor.	◆ *Come in, please.*
◆ Tome asiento por favor.	◆ *Take a seat, please.*
◆ Siéntese aquí por favor.	◆ *Please sit down here.*
◆ ¿De qué país es usted?	◆ *What country are you from?*
◆ ¿De dónde es usted?	◆ *Where are you from?*
◆ ¿Cuál es su nacionalidad?	◆ *What is your nationality?*
◆ ¿Cuántos años tiene usted?	◆ *How old are you?*
◆ ¿En qué año nació usted?	◆ *What year where you born?*
◆ ¿Cuál es su fecha de nacimiento?	◆ *What is your date of birth?*
◆ ¿Quién vive con usted?	◆ *Who lives with you?*
◆ ¿Usted vive con alguien más?	◆ *Do you live with anyone else?*
◆ ¿Tiene familiares aquí?	◆ *Do you have family members here?*
◆ ¿Cuál es su estado civil?	◆ *What is your marital status?*
◆ ¿Está usted casado/a?	◆ *Are you married?*
❯ ¿Soltera/o?	❯ *Single?*
❯ ¿Separada/o o divorciada/o?	❯ *Separated or divorced?*
❯ ¿Viuda/o?	❯ *Widowed?*

Práctica F

Read the sections of the introduction about the authors' experiences with learning a foreign language. Tell your own language-learning experiences to a small group of other learners. As you do, identify your strengths and the areas of your language competency that you wish to improve.

5. Durante la semana que viene
During the coming week

Durante la semana, practique su habilidad de evaluar a la gente entrevistando a uno de sus pacientes acerca del país o el pueblo donde nació. También pregunte sobre las cosas que son diferentes entre ese país y los Estados Unidos. Abajo, hay preguntas con que puede empezar. Añada otras que le interesan. Charle sobre lo que aprendió la próxima vez que se reúnan.

During the week, practice your assessment skills by interviewing one of your patients about the country or town where he or she was born. Ask, too, about what things are different between that country and the United States. Below are questions to begin with. Add others that interest you. Record answers in the right-hand column. Discuss what you learned the next time you meet.

Preguntas para empezar *Questions to begin with*	Respuestas de su paciente *Your patient's responses*
¿Cuál es su nacionalidad? *What is your nationality?* ¿Su país natal? *Your country of origin?* ¿De qué parte de su país viene? *From what part of your country do you come?*	
Otras preguntas que le interesan . . . *Other questions that interest you . . .*	

6. Actividades para divertirse
Activities for fun

Complete el crucigrama. Traduzca las palabras de abajo en inglés al español. Llene el crucigrama con las palabras traducidas al español.

Complete the crossword puzzle. Translate the English words listed below into Spanish. Fill the crossword with the Spanish translation.

1. Psychologist (male)
5. Sit down (formal)
6. Peru
7. Good-bye
8. He is (the verb for location)
9. Frustrated (female)

1. Country
2. Counselor (male)
3. Guatemalan (female)
4. Husband

Note: Answer key appears in the appendix.

7. En la comunidad
In the community

⧉ Vaya a la biblioteca pública para buscar libros bilingües (español e inglés) de niños que presentan las costumbres de otro país. Saque uno o dos. Mientras que está leyendo, note si hay palabras nuevas que usted llega a comprender sólo por el contexto.

☺ *Go to a local public library to look for bilingual (Spanish and English) children's books that introduce another country's customs. Check out one or two. As you read them, notice if there are new words that you can understand because of the context.*

Or

⧉ Escuche la radio en español por lo menos una hora. Haga una lista de los temas hablados y traiga la lista a la próxima sesión.

☺ *Listen to a Spanish language radio station for at least one hour. Make a list of topics discussed and bring the list to your next session.*

8. Diálogo: Esperando una vida mejor como inmigrante
Dialogue: Hoping for a better life as an immigrant

Español	English
◆ ¡Hola, buenos días!	◆ *Hello, good morning!*
▶ Buenos días.	▶ *Good morning.*
◆ ¿Cómo está usted?	◆ *How are you?*
▶ Bien gracias, ¿y usted?	▶ *Fine thanks, and you?*
◆ Bien, también.	◆ *Fine also.*
◆ Yo soy la trabajadora social.	◆ *I am the social worker.*
▶ Mucho gusto. Encantada de conocerla.	▶ *Pleased to meet you.*
◆ El gusto es mío.	◆ *The pleasure is mine.*
◆ Siéntese por favor.	◆ *Sit down, please.*
▶ Gracias.	▶ *Thank you.*

Español (continuación)	English (continued)
◆ ¿De qué país es usted?	◆ What country are you from?
▶ Soy de Guatemala.	▶ I am from Guatemala.
◆ ¿Cuántos años ha vivido en los Estados Unidos?	◆ How long have you been living in the United States?
▶ Dos años.	▶ Two years.
◆ ¿Quién vive con usted?	◆ Who lives with you?
▶ Mi esposo y mi bebé.	▶ My husband and my baby.
◆ ¿Qué tipo de trabajo hace usted?	◆ What type of work do you do?
▶ A veces, limpio casas. Pero estoy buscando un trabajo mejor.	▶ At times, I clean houses. But I am looking for more stable work.
◆ ¿Qué cosas hace difícil vivir en los Estados Unidos?	▶ What are the things that make it difficult to live in the United States?
▶ No tener dinero.	▶ Not having money.
◆ ¿Algo más?	◆ Anything else?
▶ Si, no manejar y no hablar inglés.	▶ Yes, not being able to drive and speak English.
◆ ¿Cómo le hace sentir eso?	◆ How does that make you feel?
▶ Me hace sentir frustrada y desesperada.	▶ It makes me feel frustrated and desperate.
◆ ¿Qué cosas hace para sentirse mejor?	◆ What things do you do to make yourself feel better?
▶ Hablo con mi esposo. Él me escucha mucho. También, llamo a mi mamá de vez en cuando.	▶ I talk to my husband. He is a good listener. Also, I call my mom every so often.
◆ ¿Qué más hace?	◆ What else do you do?
▶ Hablo con amigas que se sienten como yo.	▶ I talk to friends who feel the way I do.
◆ ¿Ha ido alguna vez con un especialista, como un médico, para sentirse mejor?	◆ Have you ever gone to a specialist, like a doctor, to feel better?
▶ ¡Yo no! Pero una amiga fue con un médico. Su esposo no la esuchaba y sus amigas no le entendían.	▶ Not me! But a friend of mine went to see a doctor. Her husband was not listening and her friends did not understand her.

Paso Dos

Sentimientos inesperados de depresión y tristeza

Unexpected feelings of depression and sadness

1. Para la reunión del grupo
For the group meeting

Antes de la reunión, escuche el diálogo "Preguntando sobre depresión" (http://unmpress.com/UserFiles/Audio/Spanish_for_Mental_Health_Professionals/Paso2.mp3) y lea la historia de Esperanza, la mujer de El Salvador.

Before getting together, listen to the dialogue, "Asking about depression" (http://unmpress.com/UserFiles/Audio/Spanish_for_Mental_Health_Professionals/Paso2.mp3) and read the story about Esperanza, the woman from El Salvador.

1.A. Cultura latina en contexto
Latino culture in context

"Esperanza's Migration Transition Story"

Here one lives in a gold cage, but for me, it is still a prison.

—Esperanza

About three years ago, Esperanza immigrated to North Carolina from El Salvador with her husband, José, and their son, Victor. They were grateful to have crossed the border without major problems. Shortly thereafter, Esperanza and José had a second child, a daughter. Esperanza named her "Carlota" in honor of her mother who was still in El Salvador.

The family was lucky because José found a stable job as a second shift manager at the same fast food restaurant where his brother, Hector, worked. Esperanza stayed home with her two children. They were happy that José's position paid enough to support the family's financial needs.

Recently, however, Esperanza has been feeling discouraged and dissatisfied with her life. She loves her children, now four and two years of age, but she has a feeling of emptiness, too. In El Salvador, Esperanza worked as a nurse and supported herself. Now, she has to ask José for everything. She feels too dependent on him; sometimes they don't agree on how to spend their money. Esperanza would like to get a job. But José disapproves of day care and wants her to stay with the children until they are both in school.

Esperanza misses her life in El Salvador, particularly her mother and her extended family. She has no female relatives here in the States. She is not eating regularly and is losing weight. At night she doesn't sleep well. Sometimes she cries herself to sleep. She feels sad, tired, and lacks energy. She also has frequent headaches.

She has tried to talk to José about going back to work, but he does not pay much attention to her. She talks to her friends, but they think that she complains about nothing. "José makes enough money so that you have a good life. We have to work even if we don't want to, because our husbands do not earn enough." Although Esperanza realizes that she has a "good life," as her friends say, she still feels trapped. Sometimes she feels as though she is living in a golden cage!

1.B. Charlas para empezar la reunión
Conversations to start the meeting

▦ Use su mejor español y su imaginación para describir lo que ve en la foto. Responda a las preguntas relacionadas con la foto y la historia en español o inglés. Empiece con las preguntas de abajo.

🙁 *Use your best Spanish and your imagination to describe what you see in the photograph. Answer the questions related to the story in Spanish or English. Begin with the questions below.*

a. ¿En qué tipo de comunidad cree Ud. que las señoras en la foto viven?
   In what type of community do you think the women in the photograph live?

b. ¿Qué cree Ud. que ellas hacen durante el día?
   What do you think they do during the day?

c. ¿Por qué cree Ud. que a José no le gusta una guardería para sus niños?
   Why do you think José does not like day care for his children?

d. En la historia, ¿por qué cree Ud. que Esperanza se siente deprimida?
   In the story, why do you think Esperanza feels blue (or depressed)?

e. ¿Cuáles son algunas cosas que hacen sentir a Esperanza "enjaulada"?
   What are some things that make Esperanza feel she is living in a cage?

1.C. Practique el diálogo
Practice the dialogue

▦ En grupos de dos, repase el diálogo que escuchó en este paso. Escoja un par de estudiantes para recitar el diálogo en frente del grupo.

🙁 *In groups of two, review the dialogue that you listened to for this paso. Select one pair of students to recite the dialogue in front of the group.*

2. Verbos útiles en el campo de salud mental
Useful verbs in the field of mental health

2.A. Verbos reflexivos
Reflexive verbs

En español, se usa el verbo reflexivo para hablar acerca de los sentimientos. La forma reflexiva de un verbo se usa cuando el sujeto de una oración y el objeto de un verbo son la misma persona. Esto es cuando la acción se hace a sí mismo/a. Algunos verbos, incluyendo aquéllos usados con sentimientos ya mencionados, tienen formas reflexivas y no-reflexivas. Algunos ejemplos están abajo.

In Spanish, the reflexive verb is used to talk about or express feelings. The reflexive form of a verb is used when the subject of the sentence and the object of the verb are the same. That is, a reflexive verb is used when the action is done to oneself. Some verbs, including those used for feelings mentioned earlier, have both reflexive and regular forms. Some examples are given below.

Reflexive Verb Form	Standard Verb Form
Ponerse—*to become, to get, to put on (clothing)*	poner—*to put, to place*
Sentirse—*to feel (well or ill)*	sentir—*to feel sorry, to regret, to feel*
Levantarse—*to get up, to rise*	levantar—*to lift, to raise*
Enojarse—*to become angry, to get cross*	enojar—*to make angry, to annoy*
Preguntarse—*to wonder, to ask oneself*	preguntar—*to ask, to inquire, to question*
Preocuparse—*to be concerned, to be worried*	preocupar—*to worry*
Quitarse—*to take off (one's clothes)*	quitar—*to remove (e.g., the dishes)*
Volverse loco—*to go crazy, mad*	volver—*to turn, to return*

2.B. Pronombres reflexivos
Reflexive pronouns

Los pronombres reflexivos están listados en la segunda columna en el cuadro abajo. La tercera columna presenta un ejemplo de cómo se usa el reflexivo para expresar acciones hechas por o a uno mismo.

The reflexive pronouns are listed in the second column in the table below. The third column gives an example of how the reflexive is used to express actions done by or to oneself.

Pronombres Sujetos *Subjects*	Pronombres Reflexivos *Reflexive Pronouns*	Ejemplos *Examples*
Yo *(I)*	Me *(myself, to/for myself)*	Yo no *me siento* bien; me duele la cabeza. *I don't feel well; my head hurts.*
Tú *(you)*	Te *(yourself, to/for yourself)*	¿Cómo *te sientes* hoy? ¿Mejor? *How do you feel today? Better?*
Ud. *(you, formal)*	Se *(yourself, to/for yourself)*	¿*Se pone* bravo después de beber? *Do you get angry after drinking?*
Él/Ella *(he/she)*	Se *(himself/herself, to/for himself/herself)*	Lucía *se preocupa* por su mamá que vive en Honduras. *Lucia is concerned for her mother who lives in Honduras.*
Nosotros *(we)*	Nos *(ourselves, to/for ourselves)*	*Nos fuimos* del campo por falta de trabajo. *We left the rural area due to lack of work.*
Uds. *(you, formal plural)*	Se *(yourselves, to/for yourselves)*	¿*Se preguntan* si el remedio es necesario? *You are wondering if the medicine is necessary?*
Ellos *(they)*	Se *(themselves, to/for themselves)*	Ellos casi *se vuelven* locos por falta de noticias de sus abuelos. *They are going crazy for lack of news about their grandparents.*

2.C. Los verbos "poner(se)" y "sentir(se)"
The verbs "to become," "to get," "to put" and "to feel," "to regret"

Abajo, hay dos verbos usados frecuentemente con los sentimientos. Están conjugados en el tiempo presente. Hay ejemplos de cómo usar estos verbos para expresar sentimientos. Note que los sentimientos se pueden expresar usando cuatro verbos diferentes en español: sentir, poner, ser, y estar.

Below are two verbs frequently used to express emotion. They are conjugated in the present tense. There are examples of how to use them to express feelings. Note that, in Spanish, four different verbs can be used to express feelings: to feel, to get, and to be (ser and estar).

Poner(se): *To become, to get*		Sentir(se): *To regret, to feel*	
Yo me pongo	*I become*	Yo me siento	*I feel*
Tú te pones	*You get (informal)*	Tú te sientes	*You feel (informal)*
Ud. se pone	*You get (formal)*	Ud. se siente	*You feel (formal)*
Él/Ella se pone	*He/She becomes*	Él/Ella se siente	*He/She regrets*
Nosotros nos ponemos	*We become*	Nosotros nos sentimos	*We regret*
Uds. se ponen	*You get (plural)*	Uds. se sienten	*You feel (plural)*
Ellos se ponen	*They become*	Ellos se sienten	*They regret*

■ Ponerse (*To become, to get*): *This verb may be used when a situation is perceived to cause an emotional response.*

Ejemplo/*Example*
Me pongo nervioso cuando
estoy en el consultorio del dentista.

Significado/*Meaning*
*I get nervous when
I am at the dentist's office.*

■ Sentirse (*To feel*): *The verb "to feel" is used in a similar way as in English. Almost all the adjectives that express feelings can be expressed using the verb "to feel," except when expressing pleasantness or shyness.*

Ejemplo/*Example*
¿Cómo se siente?
Me siento enojada.

Significado/*Meaning*
*How do you feel?
I feel angry.*

■ Ser (*To be*): *The use of the verb "ser" (to be) applies to enduring traits.*

Ejemplo/*Example*	Significado/*Meaning*
La niña es tímida siempre.	*The girl is always shy.*
Mis abuelos son personas felices.	*My grandparents are happy people.*

■ Estar (*To be*): *The use of the verb "estar" (to be) implies that there has been a recent change.*

Ejemplo/*Example*	Significado/*Meaning*
La niña está tímida.	*The girl feels shy right now.*
Mis abuelos están felices.	*My grandparents are happy right now.*

Práctica A

Think about patients or Latino friends who have talked with you about unexpected feelings related to their migration to the United States. Write two sentences for each verb, trying to model your words on those used by your patient or Latino friend. Explain why you chose to use the verb in each sentence.

Práctica B

In the exercise below, choose the correct pronouns to complete the phrases. Say each sentence several times until the use of the reflexive pronoun feels natural. Review section 3.B. for the vocabulary on feelings in this unit, if necessary.

1) Yo (me / te) siento deprimido porque no puedo hablar bien el inglés.
   I feel depressed because I cannot speak English well.

2) Ellos (se / me) preguntan por su amigo después del accidente.
   They are wondering about their friend after the accident.

3) Te digo, (me / te) vuelvo loco cuando el bebé llora.
   I tell you, it drives me crazy when the baby cries.

4) ¿Cómo (se / te) sientes después de hablar con tu mamá en Honduras?
   How do you feel after talking to your mother in Honduras?

5) Beatriz (me / se) levanta temprano para ir al mercado cada miércoles.
   Beatriz gets up early every Wednesday to go to the market.

6) Nosotros (nos / te) preocupamos por ti porque no comiste ayer.
   We are worried about you because you did not eat yesterday.

7) Juliana (nos / se) pone triste cuando está sola por mucho tiempo.
   Juliana becomes sad when she is alone for a long time.

8) Raúl y Pablo (se / nos) ponen bravos con nosotros cuando llegamos tarde.
   Raúl and Pablo become angry at us when we arrive late.

Práctica C

Move around the classroom. Use the questions below and the four verbs "to feel," "to become," and "to be" (ser and estar) to describe your feelings to fellow students. Remember to ask also about their country and "ciudad" or "pueblo" of birth. Practice changing from formal to informal conversation in these interviews.

Español	English
Ahora ¿cómo se siente? *(formal)* ¿cómo te sientes? *(informal)*	*How are you feeling right now?*
¿Está enojada hoy? ¿Por qué? ¿Qué pasó anoche . . . ayer?	*Are you angry today? Why? What happened last night . . . yesterday?*
¿Se pone nervioso cuando un perro se le acerca ladrando?	*Do you get nervous when a dog approaches you barking?*
¿Usted diría que usted es una persona . . . (i.e., tímida, contenta, etc.)?	*Would you say that you are a . . . (i.e., shy, content, etc.) person?*
¿Qué cosas le hacen feliz?	*What kinds of things make you happy?*

Práctica D

Think of a time when you or your family moved. How old were you? How far away did you move? What things did you anticipate with enthusiasm? . . . with hesitation? How did the move turn out? Were there situations that arose that were unexpected? How did you feel? Tell about the move and your reactions, in English or Spanish. Compare your feelings with those of your Latino patients or friends.

3. Palabras y expresiones nuevas
New words and expressions

3.A. Expresiones
Expressions

Abajo, hay una lista de saludos y despedidas más comunes. El saber usar varios de estos saludos y despedidas le ayudará a tener más confianza y seguridad con sus clientes.

Below is a list of the most commonly used greetings and farewells. Knowing several of the greetings and farewells will help you have more confidence and trust with your clients.

Saludos *Greetings*		Despedidas *Farewells*	
Hola	*Hello*	Que le vaya bien.	*Have a good day.*
Buenos días Buenas tardes Buenas noches	*Good morning Good afternoon Good evening/ night.*	Que tenga un buen día.	*Have a good day.*
¿Cómo está usted? *(formal)* ¿Cómo estás? *(informal)*	*How are you?*	Nos vemos.	*See you.*
¿Qué tal? ¿Qué pasó?	*What's up?*	Hasta luego.	*See you later.*
¿Qué hay de nuevo?	*What's new?*	Hasta pronto.	*See you soon.*
¿Cómo le va? ¿Cómo le está yendo?	*How's it going?*	Hasta la próxima. Hasta la vista.	*See you next time.*
¿Qué me cuenta?	*What can you tell me? What's going on?*	Va pues.	*Bye. (Nicaraguan)*
¿Cómo ha estado? ¿Cómo lo ha pasado?	*How have you been?*	Vaya con Diós. Adiós.	*Go with God. Good-bye.*
¿Todo bien?	*Is everything okay?*	Chao.	*Bye.*

3.B. Sentimientos
Feelings

Las palabras de abajo representan sentimientos. Note como los sentimientos son usados con los verbos "sentirse," "ponerse," "ser," y "estar."

The following words represent feelings. Note how the feelings are used with the verbs "to feel," "to become," and "to be" (ser and estar).

estar + sentimiento	
enojado/*angry*	furioso/*enraged, furious*
ser o estar + sentimiento	
agradable/*pleasant*	tímido/*shy*
estar o sentir + sentimiento	
agotado/*exhausted*	aliviado/*relieved, well*
asustado/*frightened*	cansado/*tired*
avergonzado/*ashamed*	molesto/*annoyed*
deprimido/*depressed*	enfermo/*sick*
desesperado/*desperate*	furioso/*enraged, furious*
nervioso/*nervous*	mortificado/*tormented*
preocupado/*worried*	triste/*sad (neutral)*
ser o estar o sentir + sentimiento	
agradecido/*thankful*	ansioso/*anxious*
contento/*content*	culpable/*guilty (neutral)*
frustrado/*frustrated*	feliz/*happy (neutral)*
orgulloso/*proud*	solitario/*lonely*
rechazado/*rejected*	

Most of the above words can also be used with the verb "to become" (ponerse).

Note: Each adjective can be made feminine by changing the final o to a; plurals are formed by adding an s.

3.C. Describiendo los sentimientos de otros
Describing the feelings of others

Mire las fotos de abajo. Escriba una oración corta en español que indique cómo se sienten las personas. Además, busque fotos de personas con otras expresiones. Escriba otra oración corta usando las palabras y expresiones nuevas.

Look at the pictures below. Write a short sentence in Spanish about how you think each person is feeling. Also, look in magazines for photos of people with other expressions. Write another short description using the new words and expressions.

1.

2.

3.

4.

5.

6.

Práctica E

In groups of three or four, create a role-play to practice greetings, closings, and ways of talking about feelings. Ask your client about how she feels about settling-in in the United States. If one of the other actors is a child, switch to the informal when talking with the child.

Práctica F

Write each of the feeling words above on a file card. Turn them face down. Then pick a card, read the word, and create a sentence using the word. Check to see that you have used the correct verb. Repeat, going around the group, until all of the cards have been selected.

Práctica G

Bring a set of dolls or puppets to class. Give each one a name and a family role. In groups of three, create a story about the family, using the names and roles that your group has given to them. Tell your story to the whole group. Compare stories. How do these made-up stories resemble those of your patients or Latino friends?

Práctica H

If the holiday season is near, write a short story about a family reunion or a family gathering. Include as many references as you can to as many family roles and feelings that you can think of. Don't worry if you exaggerate a bit!

3.D. Papeles en la familia
Family roles

Abajo, hay una lista de palabras que se usan con frecuencia para referirse a los familiares y parientes. Usted necesita aprender estas palabras porque su cliente latino las usará a menudo en su conversación.

Below is a list of frequently used words to refer to family and relatives. You will need to know these words because your Latino clients will use them often in conversations.

Family Roles			
Family Members	*Relatives*	*In-Laws*	*Other Members*
Madre *Mother*	Abuela *Grandmother*	Suegra *Mother-in-law*	Madrina *Godmother*
Padre *Father*	Abuelo *Grandfather*	Suegro *Father-in-law*	Padrino *Godfather*
Hermana/o *Sister/Brother*	Tía/o *Aunt/Uncle* Prima/o *Cousin*	Cuñada/o *Sister-in-law/ Brother-in-law*	Comadre *Word used by mother to refer to her child's madrina*
Hija/o *Daughter/Son* Esposa o mujer *Wife* Esposo o marido *Husband*	Nieta/o *Granddaughter/ Grandson* Sobrina/o *Niece/Nephew*	Nuera o Hija *Daughter-in-law* Yerno o Hijo político *Son-in-law*	Compadre *Word used by father to refer to his child's padrino*

4. Instrumento de evaluación: Para pacientes
Assessment tool: For patients

4.A. Instrumento de evaluación para pacientes externos
Assessment tool for outpatients

Español	English
◆ ¿Qué tiene? *(formal)* ◆ ¿Qué tienes? *(informal)*	◆ *What is the matter?*
◆ ¿Qué le pasa? ◆ ¿Qué te pasa? *(informal)*	◆ *What is the matter?* ◆ *What is happening?*
◆ ¿Cómo se siente usted? *(formal)* ◆ ¿Cómo te sientes? *(informal)*	◆ *How do you feel?*
◆ ¿Desde cuándo se siente cansada?	◆ *How long have you been feeling tired?*
◆ ¿Ha cambiado su apetito? ◆ ¿Ha perdido peso? ◆ ¿Ha aumentado de peso?	◆ *Has your appetite changed?* ◆ *Have you lost weight?* ◆ *Have you gained weight?*
◆ ¿Cuántas horas duerme cada noche?	◆ *How many hours do you sleep at night?*
◆ ¿Tiene usted problemas al dormirse? ◆ ¿Tiene usted problemas para mantenerse dormida/o?	◆ *Do you have trouble falling asleep?* ◆ *Do you have trouble staying asleep?*
◆ ¿Se siente triste o deprimida/o?	◆ *Do you feel sad or depressed?*
◆ ¿Se siente nerviosa/o?	◆ *Do you feel nervous?*
◆ ¿Llora más de lo normal?	◆ *Do you cry more than usual?*
◆ ¿Tiene pensamientos que le preocupan?	◆ *Do you have troubling thoughts?*

4.B. Instrumento de evaluación para pacientes internos
Assessment tool for inpatients

Español	English
◆ ¿Tiene pensamientos de hacerse daño? . . . o ¿Piensa en hacerse daño?	◆ *Do you ever think about hurting yourself?*
◆ ¿Tiene pensamientos de matarse? . . . o ¿Piensa en matarse?	◆ *Do you ever think about killing yourself?*
◆ ¿Matar o herir a otra persona?	◆ *Killing or hurting someone else?*
◆ ¿Oye usted voces que no oyen los demás?	◆ *Do you hear voices that others don't?*
◆ ¿Ve usted cosas que no ven los demás?	◆ *Do you see things that others don't?*
◆ ¿Cree usted que la televisión o la radio le está mandando mensajes?	◆ *Do you believe that the TV or radio is sending messages to you?*
◆ ¿Cree que alguien le persigue?	◆ *Do you think someone is following you?*
◆ ¿Cree que alguien quiere hacerle daño?	◆ *Do you think that someone is out to harm you?*
◆ ¿Ha tomado alguna medicina para los nervios?	◆ *Have you ever taken anything for your nerves?*
◆ ¿Sabe el nombre de esta medicina?	◆ *Do you know the name of this medicine?*
◆ ¿Ha hablado con un psiquiatra?	◆ *Have you ever spoken with a psychiatrist?*
◆ ¿La/lo han internado en un hospital psiquiátrico alguna vez?	◆ *Have you ever been admitted to a psychiatric hospital?*

5. Durante la semana que viene
During the coming week

Para averiguar más información sobre su cliente, use las expresiones de abajo. Escriba las respuestas en tarjetas de papel y practique esas frases durante la semana. Para la próxima clase, prepare un mini-teatro para presentar al grupo con un colega.

To find out more information about your client, use the expressions below. Write out the answers on file cards and practice repeating these sentences during the week. For the next class, prepare a mini-drama to present to the group with a colleague.

Sobre la familia Español	About the family *English*
¿Cómo se llama . . .	*What is the name of . . .*
. . . su madre?	*. . . your mother?*
. . . su padre?	*. . . your father?*
. . . su hijo/a?	*. . . your son/daughter?*
. . . su esposo/a?	*. . . your husband/wife?*
¿Cúando . . .	*When . . .*
. . . nació usted?	*. . . were you born?*
. . . nació su hijo/a?	*. . . was your son/daughter born?*
. . . fue la última vez que visitó al médico?	*. . . was the last time you visited the doctor?*
. . . es su próxima visita?	*. . . is your next visit?*
¿Quién en su familia . . .	*Who in your family . . .*
. . . tiene trabajo?	*. . . is working?*
. . . va a la escuela?	*. . . goes to school?*
. . . sabe manejar un auto?	*. . . knows how to drive?*
. . . vive con usted?	*. . . lives with you?*

6. Actividades para divertirse
Activities for fun

Complete la buscapalabras de abajo. Note, por favor, que las palabras escondidas pueden estar arregladas diagonal, vertical, o horizontalmente. Usted debe encontrar las doce palabras de abajo.

Complete the word search below. Please note that hidden words may be arranged diagonally, vertically, or horizontally. You should be able to find the twelve words below.

P	S	I	H	S	A	B	S	L	A	B	Z	E
R	C	D	E	P	P	I	T	R	I	S	T	E
E	A	N	I	E	O	E	N	O	J	A	D	O
O	N	T	E	G	N	E	N	D	Q	L	A	C
C	S	M	I	R	E	I	E	A	E	O	L	O
U	A	E	A	M	R	A	R	J	H	T	G	M
P	D	G	R	B	I	D	V	O	C	N	O	P
A	O	O	O	O	N	D	I	N	B	E	P	A
D	V	S	R	D	E	S	O	E	B	I	Q	D
A	N	R	I	T	N	E	S	E	N	T	I	R
B	M	A	D	R	I	N	A	E	S	E	H	E
D	E	P	R	I	M	I	D	O	A	M	O	N

Busque estas palabras y tradúzcalas al inglés:
Look for the following words and then translate them into English:

Cansado	Deprimido	Enojado
Compadre	Madrina	Nerviosa
Preocupada	Poner	Tímido
Triste	Sentir	Sobrino

7. En la comunidad
In the community

Mire un programa de televisión en español por lo menos por una hora. Trate de comprender el contenido del programa, prestando atención a las ideas en vez de las palabras individuales. También, note como los gestos del cuerpo y de la cara le ayudan a entender la conversación.

Watch a Spanish language television program for at least one hour. Try to understand the gist of the program by paying attention to ideas rather than individual words. Also, note how body language and facial expressions facilitate your comprehension of the conversation.

Or

Aprenda algunas palabras de una canción en español de un cassette o CD. Trate de cantar con la cantante. Cante "la, la, la" cuando tenga problemas con las palabras, pero intente cantar desde el principio hasta el fín de la canción.

Learn some of the words to a Spanish language song on cassette or CD. Try to sing along with the performer. Sing "la, la, la" when you have trouble with the words, but try to sing from the beginning to the end of the song without missing a beat.

8. Diálogo: Preguntando sobre depressión
Dialogue: Asking about depression

Español	English
◆ Buenos días. Yo soy la enfermera. ▶ Buenos días.	◆ *Good morning. I am the nurse.* ▶ *Good morning.*
◆ Yo veo que usted ha bajado de peso últimamente. ¿Come bien? ▶ No. No tengo hambre. Y, casi no como.	◆ *I see that you have lost weight recently. Are you eating well?* ▶ *No, I am not hungry. And, I hardly eat.*
◆ Usted parece estar cansada también. ¿Duerme bien? ▶ No, no duermo bien. Me siento triste. Lloro mucho. Y, tengo muchos dolores de cabeza.	◆ *You also seem to be tired? Do you sleep well?* ▶ *No, I don't sleep well. I feel sad. I cry a lot. And, I have lots of headaches.*
◆ ¿Por qué cree que se siente así? ¿Hay algo que le preocupa? ▶ Yo soy de El Salvador. Yo soy enfermera. Pero, aquí no trabajo. Y nunca salgo.	◆ *Why do you think you feel this way? Is there something that worries you?* ▶ *I am from El Salvador. I am a nurse. But, here I don't work. And, I never go out.*
◆ ¿Habla con su familia acerca de sus sentimientos? ▶ Sí, con mi marido. Pero él no me entiende.	◆ *Do you talk to your family about your feelings?* ▶ *Yes, with my husband. But, he does not really understand.*
◆ ¿Habla con otros miembros de la familia? ▶ No, porque mi mamá y mis hermanos están en El Salvador.	◆ *Do you talk to other members of your family?* ▶ *No, because my mom and my brothers and sisters are in El Salvador.*
◆ ¿Tiene amigas? ▶ Sí tengo. Pero, ellas creen que yo tengo una vida buena. Yo sé que ellas tienen razón, pero yo siento que soy inútil aquí. Yo me siento enjaulada día trás día.	◆ *Do you have friends?* ▶ *Yes, I have. But they think that I have a good life. I know they are right, but I still feel useless here. I feel like I am in a cage day after day.*

Paso Tres

Recuerdos pesados y la salud mental
Troubled memories and mental health

1. Para la reunión del grupo
For the group meeting

Antes de la reunión, escuche el diálogo "Evaluando a un paciente con el trastorno de estrés postraumático" (http://unmpress.com/UserFiles/Audio/Spanish_for_Mental_Health_Professionals/Paso3.mp3) y lea la historia sobre el Padre Juan y su congregación latina.

Before getting together, listen to the dialogue "Evaluating a patient with posttraumatic stress disorder" (http://unmpress.com/UserFiles/Audio/Spanish_for_Mental_Health_Professionals/Paso3.mp3) and read the story about Father John's experiences with his Latino congregation.

1.A. Cultura latina en contexto
Latino culture in context

"Father John's Ministry in the Latino Community"

He continuously complained of having nightmares and disturbing memories about his past.

—Father John

Father John cares for the spiritual and material needs of his Latino congregation. He offers a Spanish language Mass every Sunday afternoon. He also conducts preparation classes for marriages and baptisms and often is invited to celebrate the "quinceañera" with Latino parishioners. In addition, he has started community programs to assist with housing and employment. Sometimes parishioners come to him with their emotional needs. Father John thinks that several of the Latino men he has counseled may suffer from posttraumatic stress disorder (PTSD).

Father John believes that some of these men are in need of professional help that he cannot give. "A number of men are really traumatized, have difficult or troubling memories, and need to see a psychologist." One man from Guatemala, whom Father John remembered, had been abducted, held, and released only after his family paid a large ransom six months later. Although this man has been in the United States for two years now, he still has flashbacks of this traumatic event.

"He reports having nightmares and disturbing memories about his past. He also complains of heart palpitations when he hears a loud noise," Father John commented. He added that these men often isolate themselves because of their fear. They are afraid to go out except to go to work. They rarely go to visit friends or out for a walk as is customary in their own countries.

Father John appreciates the opportunity to help people, but he feels that some of his Latino parishioners should seek professional help. However, he realizes that the negative connotation associated with mental illness in the Latino community prevents many people from doing so.

Even when a person is willing to seek professional help, there are financial barriers. "Money is a big problem for these men. In many cases, their families depend on them financially and the men try to save every penny for their support," said Father John. He feels that his help makes a difference, but he believes that a combination of clinical therapy, medication, and spiritual counseling may be needed.

1.B. Charlas para empezar la reunión
Conversations to start the meeting

Use su mejor español y su experiencia para describir lo que ve en la foto. Responda a las preguntas relacionadas con la foto y la historia en español o inglés.

Use your best Spanish and your imagination to describe what you see in the photograph. Answer the questions related to the story in Spanish or English as best as you can.

a. ¿Qué cosas sabe usted sobre la iglesia en la vida de los latinos?
What things do you know about the church in the life of Latinos?

b. ¿Cuáles son las cosas que el Padre Juan hace para ayudar a los hombres latinos?
What are the things that Father John does to help the Latino men?

c. ¿Qué factores impiden a los hombres latinos a buscar ayuda con sus problemas de salud mental?
What factors prevent Latino men from seeking help with mental health concerns?

d. ¿Qué sugerencias tiene usted frente a las necesidades y las barreras de servicios de salud mental para los inmigrantes latinos?
What suggestions do you have for addressing the needs for and barriers to mental health service for Latino immigrants?

1.C. Practique el diálogo
Practice the dialogue

Repase el diálogo que escuchó para este paso. Ahora, en los próximos diez minutos, prepare un mini-teatro con uno de sus colegas. Preséntenlo al grupo.

Review the dialogue that you listened to for this paso. Now, in the next ten minutes, prepare a mini-drama with one of your colleagues. Present it to the group.

2. Verbos útiles en el campo de salud mental
Useful verbs in the field of mental health

2.A. El pretérito
The preterit

En español hay dos tiempos importantes que expresan una acción pasada: el pretérito y el imperfecto. El pretérito está presentado en este paso. Las reglas de uso se encuentran en el cuadro de abajo.

In Spanish there are two important tenses that express a past action: the preterit and the imperfect. This paso presents the preterit. The rules for use are found in the table below.

El pretérito
• *Expresses the beginning, end, or completion of an action.*
• *Describes an action or state within a definite time period in the past.*

Las conjugaciones para tres verbos *regulares* en el pretérito se encuentran en el cuadro de abajo. Note que los infinitivos en español terminan en "-ar," "-er," o "-ir." Hay un ejemplo de cada uno.

The past tense conjugations for three regular verbs are found in the table below. Notice that infinitive verbs in Spanish end in "-ar," "-er," or "-ir." An example of each is given; the endings used in the preterit are italicized.

Ayudar—*to help*	Temer—*to fear*	Sentir—*to regret, to feel*
Yo ayud*é*	Yo tem*í*	Yo sent*í*
Tú ayud*aste*	Tú tem*iste*	Tú sent*iste*
Ud./usted ayud*ó*	Ud./usted tem*ió*	Ud./usted sint*ió*
Él/Ella ayud*ó*	Él/Ella tem*ió*	Él/Ella sint*ió*
Nosotros ayud*amos*	Nosotros tem*imos*	Nosotros sent*imos*
Uds./ustedes ayud*aron*	Uds./ustedes tem*ieron*	Uds./ustedes sint*ieron*
Ellos/Ellas ayud*aron*	Ellos/Ellas tem*ieron*	Ellos/Ellas sint*ieron*

En el cuadro siguiente, usted encontrará las conjugaciones de los verbos presentados en paso 1. Note que "ser," "estar," y "tener" son verbos irregulares en sus formas del pretérito.

In the table below, you will find the conjugations of the verbs presented in paso 1. Notice that "ser," "estar," and "tener" are irregular in their preterite form.

"Must-know" verbs

Ser—*to be*	Estar—*to be*	Tener—*to have*
Yo fu*i*	Yo estuv*e*	Yo tuv*e*
Tú fu*iste*	Tú estuv*iste*	Tú tuv*iste*
Ud./usted fu*e*	Ud./usted estuvo	Ud./usted tuvo
Él/Ella fu*e*	Él/Ella estuvo	Él/Ella tuvo
Nosotros fu*imos*	Nosotros estuv*imos*	Nosotros tuv*imos*
Uds./ustedes fu*eron*	Uds./ustedes estuv*ieron*	Uds./ustedes tuv*ieron*
Ellos/Ellas fu*eron*	Ellos/Ellas estuv*ieron*	Ellos/Ellas tuv*ieron*

Práctica A

Give the Spanish or English equivalent in the past tense of the verb phrases below.

They helped _____   Temimos _____

He was _____   Nosotros ayudamos _____

We went _____   Uds. sintieron _____

I felt _____   Yo estuve _____

You feared _____   Ella fue _____

She put _____   Tú sentiste _____

Práctica B

In the blank to the right of the sentences, fill in the correct form of the preterit.

1) Ayer, (visitar) a tres personas recién llegadas de México. *Yesterday, I visited three people who just arrived from Mexico.*	
2) La oficina (tener) tres consultorios privados. *The office had three private consulting rooms.*	
3) Una vez, yo (hablar) con un señor de Colombia. *Once, I talked with a man from Colombia.*	
4) Se (sentir) feliz después de hablar con su mamá. *She felt happy after talking with her mother.*	

3. Palabras y expresiones nuevas
New words and expressions

3.A. Síntomas
Symptoms

Abajo, hay una lista de síntomas que un cliente con problemas de la salud mental puede sentir.

Below is a list of symptoms that a client with mental health problems could feel.

Español	English
Desmayos	Fainting
Debilidad de las manos o las manos se duermen	Numbness or weakness of the hands
Dolor de cabeza	Headache
Dolor del cuerpo en general	Generalized body pains
Calor del pecho que sube a la cabeza, o "los calores"	Heat in the chest rising to the head
El delirio	Delirium
El llanto	Sobbing
Gritar, jurar, o golpear	Shouting, swearing, or striking out
Insomnio	Insomnia
Irritabilidad	Irritability
La falta de apetito	Lack of appetite
Las alucinaciones	Hallucinations
La paranoia	Paranoia
La tristeza	Sadness
Las voces	Voices
Las palpitaciones del corazón	Heart palpitations
La preocupación	Worry
Tembloroso	Trembling

3.B. Medicinas
Medicines

Abajo, hay una lista de tipos de medicinas y remedios caseros más comunes que se usan para tratar enfermedades emocionales.

Below is a list of types of medicines and home remedies commonly used to treat emotional illnesses.

Tipos de medicinas Español	Types of medicines English
antidepresivos	*antidepressants*
calmantes	*sedatives*
hipnóticos	*hypnotics*
inyección	*injection*
jarabe	*syrup/elixir*
antipsicótico	*antipsychotic*
pastillas o píldoras	*pills*
tranquilizante	*tranquilizer*
hierbas	*herbs*
té o mate (de hierba), té de manzanilla	*tea or herbal tea, chamomile (or "sleepy time") tea*

3.C. Palabras interrogativas
Question words

Esta lista tiene palabras interrogativas. Diga estas palabras. Luego, abajo de cada uno, escriba dos preguntas que usted le puede hacer a un cliente relacionadas con la salud mental.

This list contains interrogative words. Say these words out loud. Then, below each one, write two mental health–related questions that you could ask a client.

¿Quién/Quiénes? *Who?* _____

_____

¿Qué? *What?* _____

_____

¿Cómo? *How?* _____

_____

¿Dónde? *Where?* _____

_____

¿Por qué? *Why?* _____

_____

¿Cuándo? *When?* _____

_____

¿Cuál/Cuáles? *Which?* _____

_____

Práctica C
With a partner, take turns being the priest or minister and a member of your community who is troubled by events that happened before or during migration. Ask and respond to questions that would help you have a better understanding of the reasons for this individual's "feelings of blueness" or sadness or anxiety.

Práctica D
Now, with a partner, write a dialogue of at least ten sentences using some of these expressions and verbs from the first three pasos. Then, draw a simple picture to illustrate the dialogue that you wrote. If necessary, use a combination of Spanish and English in the dialogue to more accurately express your concerns and worries.

Práctica E

To relax and practice this new vocabulary, play this game. Think of a word given in the list of new words and expressions. Write one dash on a flip chart or other piece of paper for every letter of the word. Ask your group members to guess the letters in the word. Write them in as they guess a letter correctly. Keep track of how many letters are guessed before the word is complete. See how few guesses are necessary to complete the word. When the word is complete, use it correctly in a sentence. Repeat until everyone in the group has suggested a word.

Práctica F

Some of the words in the dialogue are included among the Memory Cards provided in the appendix. Take some time to write other words or phrases that you need to practice on file cards or card stock. If you copy the Memory Card design back onto sheets of card stock before writing new words, you can make more matching cards for an expanded memory game!

Práctica G

Often, we avoid learning new words because the pronunciation is difficult or the accent falls on a different syllable than the cognate, or similar word in English. While language learning is a cognitive process, language pronunciation is essentially mechanical. When confronted with a list of new words or phrases, repeat each word over and over again—five or ten times. Notice how much more able the muscles of your cheeks, mouth, and lips are to copy the sound and the rhythm of the words or phrases after such repetition.

4. Instrumento de evaluación: Preguntas para evaluar la presencia de PTSD

Assessment tool: Questions to evaluate the presence of PTSD

Español	English
◆ ¿Le ha pasado o ha visto algo traumático en su vida? ▶ Sí . . . o . . . no.	◆ *Have you experienced or seen traumatic events?* ▶ *Yes . . . or . . . no.*
◆ ¿Qué tipo de síntomas tiene?	◆ *What kinds of symptoms do you have?*
◆ ¿Ha estado en una guerra civil?	◆ *Have you been in a civil war?*
◆ ¿Ha visto un asesinato o un homicidio?	◆ *Have you seen an assassination or a murder?*
◆ ¿Ha perdido un miembro de su familia en un huracán o un terremoto?	◆ *Have you lost a family member in a hurricane or an earthquake?*
◆ ¿Ha estado en o ha visto un accidente terrible? ¿ . . . con un carro, camión, u otro objeto?	◆ *Have you been in or seen a terrible accident? . . . with a car, truck, or other object?*
◆ ¿Le molestan todavía los recuerdos de estos eventos?	◆ *Do the memories of these events still bother you?*
◆ ¿Hay cosas que ve usted que otros no ven?	◆ *Are there things that you see that others don't see?*
◆ ¿Hay voces que le molestan? ¿Cuándo? ¿Qué dicen las voces?	◆ *Are there voices that bother you? When? What do they say?*
◆ ¿Tiene pesadillas? ¿Qué clase de pesadillas? ¿Frecuentemente o raramente?	◆ *Do you have nightmares? What kind of nightmares? Frequently or rarely?*

Práctica H

Think of a troubling moment in your life or in that of a close friend. Identify the event or events that were troubling. In as much detail as you can, describe feelings you had and how they affected day-to-day events. Then, think about whom you talked with or what you did that was helpful to put the feelings in perspective. Share part of your reflection with the group.

5. Durante la semana que viene
During the coming week

Vaya a su farmacia local y busque algunas medicinas con direcciones de uso en español e inglés. Después, pregúntele a la farmacéutica si ella o él puede imprimir direcciones de recetas en español para pacientes latinos.

Go to your local pharmacy and see if there are any medicines that give directions for use in Spanish and English. Then, ask the pharmacist if she or he can print directions for prescriptions in Spanish for Latino patients.

Or

Vaya al World Wide Web y lea algunos sitios que tratan sobre la salud mental. Abajo, hay algunos sitios para empezar. Si encuentra otros, mándelos a los miembros de su grupo por correo electrónico o tráigalos a la próxima clase.

Go to the World Wide Web and visit sites that discuss mental health. Below are some places to begin. If you find others, send them to the members of your group by e-mail or bring them to the next class.

CDC en español, salud mental
http://www.cdc.gov/spanish/mental.htm

The Boston Women's Health Book Collective, Nuestros cuerpos,
      nuestras vidas: Guía de capacitación para promotoras de salud
http://www.ourbodiesourselves.org/promo.htm

San Antonio Public Library: Latino: Curanderismo
*(folk beliefs and practices in mental health; espiritismo; complementary
      approaches to traditional mental health)*
www.sat.lib.tx.us/Latino/curand.htm

6. Actividades para divertirse
Activities for fun

▰ Empiece una conversación con uno de sus clientes sobre sus parientes, sus fiestas, o sus comidas típicas. Pregúntele qué cosas extraña más de su país. Pregúntele cómo celebran esas fiestas aquí y si hay algunas comidas nativas en los supermercados "americanos."

Start a conversation with one of your clients about his extended family, holidays, or typical foods. Ask about what types of things from his country he misses the most. Ask how they celebrate the holidays here and if there are any of their native foods in American supermarkets.

Or

▰ En las últimas páginas del libro, encontrará tarjetas de Memoria. Usando las instrucciones, haga un grupo de tarjetas. Juegue unos partidos de Memoria con otro miembro del grupo para practicar las frases y el vocabulario. Continúe el juego con tarjetas de Memoria hechas de otros pasos.

In the back of the book you will find Memory Cards. Using the instructions, make a set of cards. Play a few games of Memory with another group member to practice the sentences and vocabulary. Continue the game with cards made from other pasos.

7. En la comunidad
In the community

▰ Vaya a un restaurante que sirve comida latina y observe la interacción de una familia latina. Observe las expresiones faciales, la postura corporal, y los gestos. Luego escriba una nota breve sobre su observación enfocando en los siguientes factores.

1. Desarrolle una teoría acerca de lo que está pasando.
2. Examine pistas disponibles, luego tome nota de las que influyen más en su interpretación.
3. Comparta sus observaciones, usando su español, con un amigo.

Go to a restaurant that serves Latino food and observe a Latino family interact. Observe facial expressions, posture, and gestures. Then write a brief note on your observation focusing on these three factors.

1. *Develop a theory about what is going on.*
2. *Examine available clues, then take note of the ones that influence your interpretation.*
3. *Share your observations, using your Spanish, with a friend.*

8. Diálogo: Evaluando a un paciente con el trastorno de estrés postraumático
Dialogue: Evaluating a patient with posttraumatic stress disorder

Español	English
◆ Buenos días. ▶ Buenos días, Doctor.	◆ *Good morning.* ▶ *Good morning, Doctor.*
◆ ¿Qué lo trae aquí? ▶ El Padre Juan me dijo que debía venir a hablarle.	◆ *What brings you here?* ▶ *Father John told me that I ought to come talk to you.*
◆ Sí, el Padre Juan me habló que usted vendría a verme. ▶ El insistió tanto que tuve que cumplir.	◆ *Yes, Father John told me that you would come to see me.* ▶ *He insisted so much that I had to agree.*
◆ Soy el Doctor Smith, el psiquiatra. ▶ Me llamo Jorge Castillo-Reyes.	◆ *I am Dr. Smith, the psychiatrist.* ▶ *My name is Jorge Castillo-Reyes.*
◆ ¿Qué le pasa? ▶ Tengo pesadillas y no puedo dormir en la noche.	◆ *What is troubling you?* ▶ *I have nightmares and I cannot sleep at night.*
◆ ¿Qué más le pasa? ▶ Tengo palpitaciones del corazón y escucho voces.	◆ *What else have you experienced?* ▶ *I have heart palpitations and I hear voices.*
◆ ¿Qué dicen las voces? ▶ Me dicen que me van a matar.	◆ *What do the voices say?* ▶ *They say that they are going to kill me.*

Español (continuación)	English (continued)
◆ ¿Ve cosas que otra persona no puede ver?	◆ *Do you see things that others don't see?*
▶ No, Doctor.	▶ *No, Doctor.*
◆ ¿Le ha pasado o ha visto un evento traumático?	◆ *Have you experienced or seen a traumatic event?*
▶ Sí, cuando estaba en Guatemala.	▶ *Yes, when I was in Guatemala.*
◆ ¿Qué pasó en Guatemala?	◆ *What happened in Guatemala?*
▶ Me secuestraron por seis meses.	▶ *I was abducted for six months.*
◆ Debe haber sido una experiencia muy difícil para usted.	◆ *It must have been a very difficult experience for you.*
▶ Sí, Doctor. Después que me soltaron, no podía salir de mi casa porque temía que me secuestrarían otra vez.	▶ *Yes, Doctor. After they freed me, I could not leave my house because I was afraid that they would abduct me again.*
◆ Y ahora ¿con qué frecuencia sale usted de su casa?	◆ *And now, how often do you leave your house?*
▶ Solamente para ir a trabajar.	▶ *Only to go to work.*
▶ De vez en cuando visito a mi sobrina. Ella tiene un hijo de dos años y medio.	▶ *Once in a while, I visit my niece. She has a two-and-a-half-year-old son.*
◆ ¿Teme que lo secuestren otra vez?	◆ *Are you afraid that they will abduct you again?*
▶ Pues no, porque ahora vivo en los Estados Unidos. Pero todavía no me siento cómodo saliendo. No sé cómo explicarle. Me siento mejor en casa.	▶ *Well no, because now I live in the United States. But I still do not feel comfortable going out. I don't know how to explain it. I feel better at home.*
◆ Le voy a recetar un medicamento. Esto lo hará sentir mejor. Tome este medicamento. Y, vuelva a verme en dos semanas.	◆ *I will prescribe a medication. This will make you feel better. Take the medicine. And come see me after two weeks.*
▶ Gracias, doctor.	▶ *Thank you, Doctor.*
◆ Además de tomar las pastillas, le recomiendo que coma bien, y duerma ocho horas por la noche. Ejercicio regular es bueno, también. Quizás, si pasa más tiempo con el hijo de su sobrina, le ayudará también.	◆ *In addition to taking the pills, I recommend that you eat well and sleep eight hours every night. Exercise is good, also. Maybe, if you spend more time with your niece's son, it will help you, too.*
▶ Sí, Doctor. El chiquito me hace feliz.	▶ *Yes, Doctor. The little one makes me happy.*

Paso Cuatro

El fin de semana: Alcohol y carros
The weekend: Alcohol and cars

1. Para la reunión del grupo
For the group meeting

![icon] Antes de la reunión, escuche el diálogo "La semana próxima: Entrevista con el consejero de abuso de sustancias" (http://unmpress.com/UserFiles/Audio/Spanish_for_Mental_Health_Professionals/Paso4.mp3) y lea la historia que cuenta Guillermina sobre un fin de semana con amigos.

Before getting together, listen to the dialogue "The next week: Interview with the substance abuse counselor" (http://unmpress.com/UserFiles/Audio/Spanish_for_Mental_Health_Professionals/Paso4.mp3) and read the story that Guillermina tells about a weekend with friends.

1.A. Cultura latina en contexto
Latino culture in context

"Raúl's Weekend with His Friends"

Here is my husband and two friends. They came to watch TV. They are single. Here there is nothing for single people to do.
                                                            —*Guillermina*

Raúl, Luis, and Carlos work together in a factory where small electric motors are assembled. They became friends while sharing their passion for cars. Luis and Carlos are single. Raúl is married. Luis and Carlos often come over to Raúl's place, especially on the weekends. Sometimes, on Saturday afternoons, they work on their cars. Other times, they relax and watch the Latin American soccer matches on television. They have a beer or two and trade stories about their favorite players.

"They come to our house a lot," says Guillermina, Raúl's wife. "I enjoy having them over. I feel badly that there are no other fun places for them to go. In our town, everybody hung out at the plaza—especially on Sunday afternoons." Raúl is happy when the three young friends get together. "I think it reminds him of our life in Michoacán in central Mexico," says Guillermina. "In my country, we used to walk over to Raúl's father's house on the weekend. These gatherings were usually filled with lots of good food, music, and plenty of cervezas." Drinking was not a problem there because people usually stayed over after the party. "All the men drank too much at these parties, but we always stayed over at my in-laws until the next day when the men were sober and we could all walk home together."

A couple of weeks ago there was a soccer match on Sunday evening. Luis and Carlos came by to cheer for Mexico and had couple of drinks with Raúl. Later that night, they left to drive home because they needed to be ready for work early on Monday morning. "We told them they should stay over, but they said that they needed to go to work early." On the way home, Luis was stopped by the police. He had forgotten to wear his seatbelt. He also had an open beer bottle in the car. The police arrested Luis and took his driver's license away.

Later, Luis was assigned to meet with a substance abuse counselor for six weeks. Guillermina acknowledges that this was not a pleasant experience for Luis. She is relieved that no one was hurt, however. She admits that the incident made each of them more aware of the potential danger and the legal consequences of drinking and driving in the United States.

1.B. Charlas para empezar la reunión
Conversations to start the meeting

⬛ Use su mejor español y su imaginación para describir lo que ve en la foto. Responda a las preguntas relacionadas con la historia en español o inglés. Empiece con las preguntas de abajo.

🙁 *Use your best Spanish and your imagination to describe what you see in the photograph. Answer the questions related to the story in Spanish or English as best you can. Begin with the questions below.*

a. ¿Quiénes son las personas en la foto?
 Who are the people in the photograph?

b. ¿Dónde están ellos? ¿Qué hacen?
 Where are they? What are they doing?

c. ¿Cómo cree Ud. que se sienten ellos?
 How do you think they feel?

d. En la historia, ¿qué hacen Luis y Carlos los fines de semana?
 In the story, what do Luis and Carlos do on weekends?

e. ¿Qué le pasó a Luis un domingo después de tomar mucho?
 What happened to Luis one Sunday after drinking?

1.C. Practique el diálogo
Practice the dialogue

⬛ En grupos de dos, repase el diálogo que escuchó en este paso. Escoja un par de estudiantes para recitar el diálogo en frente del grupo. Trate de modificar el diálogo usando palabras que ha aprendido en este curso o de sus pacientes.

🙁 *In groups of two, review the dialogue that you listened to for this paso. Select one pair of students to recite the dialogue in front of the group. Try to modify the dialogue using words that you have learned in this course or from your patients.*

2. Verbos útiles en el campo de salud mental
Useful verbs in the field of mental health

2.A. El tiempo imperfecto
The imperfect tense

El tiempo imperfecto es el segundo tiempo importante que expresa una acción pasada. Las reglas para su uso se encuentran en el cuadro de abajo.

The imperfect tense is the second important tense that expresses action in the past. The rules for its use are found in the table below.

El imperfecto
• *Tells what was going on*
• *Expresses how things used to be*
• *Used for descriptions of persons or things in the past*
• *Used for telling time in the past*

En la página proxima, hay dos verbos conjugados en el tiempo imperfecto. Se usan ambos verbos con frecuencia en relación al alcohol, aunque, también, pueden ser usados en otros contextos. Note la diferencia entre la terminación de los verbos "-ar" y "-er." Los que terminan en "-ir" usan las mismas terminaciones que los verbos en "-er. "

On the next page are the imperfect tense conjugations for two verbs. Both verbs are used frequently in reference to alcohol, though they may be used in other contexts, too. Notice the difference in the endings for the "-ar" verbs and the "-er" verbs; "-ir" verbs use the same endings as the "-er" verbs.

Tomar—to have (something to eat or drink), to take		Beber—to drink	
Yo tom*aba*	*I was drinking*	Yo beb*ía*	*I was drinking*
Tú tom*abas* (informal)	*You were drinking (informal)*	Tú beb*ías*	*You were drinking*
Ud. tom*aba* (formal)	*You were drinking*	Ud. beb*ía*	*You were drinking*
Él/Ella tom*aba*	*He/She was drinking (formal)*	Él/Ella beb*ía*	*He/She was drinking*
Nosotros tom*ábamos*	*We were drinking*	Nosotros beb*íamos*	*We were drinking*
Uds. tom*aban*	*You were drinking (plural)*	Uds. beb*ían*	*You were drinking (plural)*
Ellos tom*aban*	*They were drinking*	Ellos beb*ían*	*They were drinking*

Práctica A

In the exercise below, write the correct form of the suggested verb in the imperfect tense on the blank. Remember to place accents where appropriate.

1) Los amigos (beber) algunas cervezas en la tarde. _____

2) Usted (usar) la marijuana hasta hace poco. _____

3) Yo (tomar) vino con mis amigos en los días de fiesta. _____

4) Los amigos (dormir) hasta mediodía. _____

5) Raúl, Luis, y Carlos (mirar) el fútbol todos los sábados. _____

6) Guillermina se (sentir) confundida de las leyes de aquí. _____

7) Ella (comer) la cena con sus amigos los fines de semana. _____

8) Él (estar) manejando demasiado rápido en la calle. _____

🔲 Recuerde que "ser" es un verbo irregular en el tiempo imperfecto. Aquí, usted encuentra la conjugación de este verbo y los verbos "estar" y "tener" los cuáles son también usados frecuentemente.

😐 *Remember that "ser" is an irregular verb in the imperfect. Here, you will find the conjugation of this verb as well as "estar" and "tener," which are also used frequently.*

Irregular verbs Ser—*to be*	Estar—*to be*	Tener—*to have*
Yo er*a*	Yo est*aba*	Yo ten*ía*
Tú er*as*	Tú est*abas*	Tú ten*ías*
Ud. er*a*	Ud. est*aba*	Ud. ten*ía*
Él/Ella er*a*	Él/Ella est*aba*	Él/Ella ten*ía*
Nosotros ér*amos*	Nosotros est*ábamos*	Nosotros ten*íamos*
Uds. er*an*	Uds. est*aban*	Uds. ten*ían*
Ellos/Ellas er*an*	Ellos/Ellas est*aban*	Ellos/Ellas ten*ían*

Práctica B

Circle the correct response for each sentence. The tenses presented include: the present, the preterit, and the imperfect. Explain your choice in the blank at right.

Hoy, no me (siento / sentía) bien porque tengo fiebre.	
La semana pasada me (siento / sentía) feliz después de hablar con mi mamá.	
Él (tomó / tomaba) demasiada cerveza cuando era joven.	
Los hombres (limpiaron / limpian) sus carros ayer.	
Las mujeres (cocinan / cocinaron) juntas en todas las fiestas el año pasado.	
En la corte, el juez siempre (tiene / tuvo) que evaluar los hechos.	

Práctica C

Unscramble the words in the second and fourth columns, writing the verb form in the preterit or imperfect on the line. The verb, in the infinitive form, in the first column is a clue.

		El pretérito		El imperfecto
Beber	ionbbere	_____	abíbne	_____
Tomar	óomt	_____	mbatao	_____
Poner	seup	_____	aípnno	_____
Estar	ssetitevu	_____	teasab	_____
Fumar	rumnafo	_____	ambsauf	_____
Juzgar	ztugseaj	_____	najzaubg	_____

2.B. Modismos
Idiomatic expressions

En español, hay muchos modismos formados con verbos básicos. El verbo es conjugado como cualquier otro verbo. Aquí hay algunos ejemplos que son útiles al hablar con sus clientes. Termine las frases de abajo.

In Spanish, there are many idioms—expressions with unpredictable meanings—formed with basic verbs. The verb is conjugated just like any other verb. Here are some that are useful in talking with your clients. Finish the sentences below.

1. Acabar de + infinitive (to have just + infinitive)
   Ej: Yo acabo de tomar seis cervezas. (I just drank six beers.)

2. Hacer daño (to hurt)
   Yo _____

3. Tener la culpa (to be to blame)
   Ud. _____

4. Echar la culpa (to put or lay the blame on)
   Nosotros_____

5. Darse cuenta de (to realize)
   Ellos_____

3. Palabras y expresiones nuevas
New words and expressions

3.A. Uso de alcohol
Alcohol use

Aquí hay una lista de palabras relacionadas con el alcohol y su uso. Estas palabras le pueden ayudar a comunicar mejor con sus clientes.

Here is a list of words related to alcohol and its use. These words can help you communicate better with your clients.

Español	English
las bebidas *("refrescos" refers to carbonated beverages)*	*drinks (of alcohol)*
el vino, "tinto"	*wine, red wine*
la cerveza	*beer*
un trago	*a shot of hard liquor*
las sustancias, substancias	*substances*
un borracho / una borracha	*a drunkard*
estar borracho	*to be drunk*
manejar bajo la influencia del alcohol	*driving while impaired*
la máquina para analizar el aliento	*Breathalyzer (machine)*
un examen de aliento	*Breathalyzer test*
un chequeo de orina	*urine check/screening*
la corte, el juez	*court, judge*
la escuela de tránsito de alcoholismo y drogadicción	*alcohol and drug education traffic school*
suspensión de la licencia de conducir	*driver's license suspension*

3.B. Sustancias
Substances

Note las diferentes maneras de llamar las drogas y sus usos, incluyendo el "slang" en esta lista de palabras.

Note the different ways of talking about the drugs and their uses, including slang, in this list of words related to the use of drugs.

Español	El Slang, El Argot / *Slang*	English
la marijuana	la yerba, el zacate	*marijuana*
la mota	la lechuga, la marimba	*pot*
un pito	un chivo	*joint*
la cocaína	la coca	*cocaine, coke*
las rocas de coca	el crack	*crack*
la heroína	la hera, la manteca	*heroin*
adicto	el molleto, el mosquero, el tecado	*an addict*
drogarse	empullarse	*to shoot up*
la jeringa	la pistola	*a syringe*
una aguja	un aparato	*needle*

Práctica D

Now think of some additional slang words related to alcohol or drug use that you have heard. Tell what standard word is the equivalent of the slang word and explain the origins of the slang word. Give an example or two of how it is used in context. Give as much of your explanation as possible in Spanish.

Práctica E

Play "A day in the life of . . ." As a group, tell a story in Spanish of a day in the life of Raúl or Guillermina. In turn, each member of the group should add a sentence, expanding and embellishing the story. Try to practice verb tenses and use new vocabulary in telling your part of the story. Tell the story until it is complete—or the day has ended. The story begins: "Raúl (or Guillermina) se levanta a las seis de la mañana para tomar el desayuno."

Práctica F

Practice conjugating verbs by number (singular or plural) or person (I, you [informal, formal], he, she, it, we, or you [plural]) by answering the following questions in the appropriate tense:

1. ¿Quién bebe la cerveza los sábados?

   a.Yo _____   d. Nosotros _____

   b.Tú _____   e. Ellos, Ellas, Uds. _____

   c.Él, Ella, Ud. _____

2. ¿Quién era el psicólogo de Argentina? *(Repeat as in previous question.)*

3. ¿Quién hablaba cada domingo con su mamá? *(Repeat as in previous question.)*

4. ¿Quién fue a la escuela de ESL (English as a Second Language) la semana pasada? *(Repeat as in previous question.)*

Práctica G

Make a visit to your local department of motor vehicles, the county courthouse, the police station, or other local governmental organization. Ask for materials in Spanish—like those that would be given to a Latino who asked for them. Tell the receptionist of your interest in learning Spanish related to mental health and law enforcement.

Review the materials. Do they appear to be appropriate in terms of grade level and culture? Read the materials aloud to yourself or a colleague; listen to the rhythm of the language. Listen for the use of reflexives, the choice of verb tense, and adjective-noun agreement. Make cards for yourself when there is new vocabulary.

Report to your group on what you found and learned!

3.C. Ampliando su vocabulario: Números, fechas, y meses
Expanding your vocabulary: Numbers, dates, and months

Esta sección le provee el vocabulario que usted puede usar en la oficina para hacer citas y llamadas telefónicas, mandar cuentas, y otras cosas. Practique su pronunciación en voz alta.

This section provides you with the vocabulary you can use for making appointments and telephone calls, sending bills, and other things. Practice your pronunciation out loud.

Números/*Numbers*

1—uno	11—once	30—treinta	1st—primero/a
2—dos	12—doce	40—cuarenta	2nd—segundo/a
3—tres	13—trece	50—cincuenta	3rd—tercero/a
4—cuatro	14—catorce	60—sesenta	4th—cuarto/a
5—cinco	15—quince	70—setenta	5th—quinto/a
6—seis	16—diez y seis	80—ochenta	6th—sexto/a
7—siete	17—diez y siete	90—noventa	7th—séptimo/a
8—ocho	18—diez y ocho	100—cien	8th—octavo/a
9—nueve	19—diez y nueve	200—doscientos	9th—noveno/a
10—diez	20—veinte	300—trescientos	10th—décimo/a

Las estaciones y meses / *The seasons and months*

invierno	primavera	verano	otoño
diciembre	marzo	junio	septiembre
December	*March*	*June*	*September*
enero	abril	julio	octubre
January	*April*	*July*	*October*
febrero	mayo	agosto	noviembre
February	May	*August*	*November*

Práctica H

Pick a partner. Role-play the receptionist and a family member. Ask the family member for the date of birth for each member of the family. It is a large family! The numbers "mil" (1,000), "dos mil" (2,000), and "novecientos" (900) will be useful to you in naming the year of birth. For example, the adult family member may have been born in "mil novecientos setenta y seis," but a young child may have been born in "dos mil dos." Practice naming years until the words are easy to say.

Práctica I

Playing Lingo is a fun way to practice the names of numbers, months, and seasons. Below is a model of a game card. Make other similar cards—everyone should have a different card—put the answers on card stock, and cut enough extra blank pieces to be able to cover the squares of each player's card. Call out the answers in English. Place a marker on the Spanish equivalent. Call "Lingo" when you get five across, down, or diagonally. Try to memorize the words as you play.

L	I	N	G	O
primavera	diez y ocho	cuatro	once	diciembre
veinte y siete	invierno	ochenta y cinco	treinta y tres	sesenta y siete
seis	enero	*libre*	agosto	cuarenta y dos
mayo	cincuenta	cien	otoño	febrero
diez	siete	setenta y seis	quince	verano

4. Instrumento de evaluación: Abuso de alcohol y drogas
Assessment tool: Alcohol and drug abuse

Español	English
¿Toma bebidas alcohólicas? ¿Cuántas bebidas toma al día? ¿Con qué frecuencia?	*Do you drink? How many drinks do you have in a day? How often?*
¿Bebe usted durante la semana? O, ¿toma solamente los fines de semana?	*Do you drink during the week? Or, do you drink only on weekends?*
¿Cuándo empezó a beber? ¿En los EE.UU. o en México (o en su país de origen)?	*When did you begin to drink? Here in the United States or in Mexico (in home country)?*
¿Ha recibido un chequeo de orina?	*Have you had your urine screened?*
¿Le han hecho un examen de aliento?	*Have you had a Breathalyzer test?*
¿Usa drogas u otras sustancias ilegales? . . . ¿cocaína? . . . ¿heroína?	*Do you use drugs or other illegal substances? . . . cocaine? . . . heroin?*
¿Fuma marijuana?	*Do you smoke marijuana?*
¿Toma bebidas o usa drogas en secreto? Es decir, solo, sin decirle a nadie.	*Do you drink or use drugs in secret? That is, alone, without telling anyone.*
¿Le han arrestado por manejar bajo la influencia del alcohol?	*Have you been arrested for driving under the influence of alcohol?*
¿Tuvo que ir a la corte y ver a un juez?	*Have you gone to a court and seen a judge?*
¿Le suspendieron su licencia de manejar?	*Did you have your driver's license suspended?*
¿Le han recomendado algún programa de tratamiento por sus problemas con el uso de alcohol o droga?	*Have you been recommended for any treatment programs for alcohol or drug-related problems?*
¿Usted ha aceptado este tratamiento? ¿Cómo le fue? ¿Terminó el programa?	*Did you accept this treatment? How did it go? Did you complete the program?*

Práctica J

In the box, you will see some words relevant to the court system. Put these words in sentences or questions using the dialogue from paso 4 as a guide.

Abogado *Lawyer*	
Alcohol *Alcohol*	
Libertad condicional *Probation*	
Tratamiento *Treatment*	
Mandado por la corte *Court ordered*	

Práctica K

Using your knowledge of the present, the preterit, and the imperfect, choose the correct verb conjugation to complete the following sentences.

1. Usted (fuma / fumó) la marijuana ayer sabiendo que es ilegal.
   You smoked marijuana yesterday knowing that it is illegal.

2. Yo no (uso / usaba) drogas ahora.
   I am not using drugs now.

3. El juez (tuvo / tiene) que suspender mi licencia de manejar el mes pasado.
   The judge had to suspend my driver's license last month.

4. Nosotros (tomamos / tomábamos) cervezas en el partido de fútbol esta tarde.
   We drank beer at the soccer game this afternoon.

5. Tomás (comparte / compartía) todo lo que tiene.
   Tomás shares everything that he has.

6. Raúl (vivía / vivió) en México cuando era niño.
   Raúl was living in Mexico when he was a child.

5. Durante la semana que viene
During the coming week

Una forma de aprender palabras nuevas relacionadas con su trabajo es pensar en situaciones en las cuales usted quiere decir algo pero no puede. Piense en barreras comunes al uso de servicios de la salud. Estas pueden ser relacionadas con la falta de conocimiento del servicio, dificultades de conseguir transporte, horas de trabajo, cuidado de niños, u otras circunstancias socio-económicas. Otras barreras pueden ser relacionadas con vergüenza.

Organice una lista de vocabulario que le puede ayudar a hablar con un cliente sobre estas barreras y escriba las palabras en inglés en unas tarjetas de índice. Busque la traducción apropiada en español y escríbala al otro lado de la tarjeta. Haga, por lo menos, veinte y cinco tarjetas nuevas. Cuando usted encuentre una palabra nueva la cual le gustaría usar con sus clientes, añádala a esta colección de vocabulario.

One way to gain new work-related vocabulary is to think about a situation and the words that you want to say but cannot. Think about some familiar barriers to the use of health-care services. These may be related to lack of knowledge of services, difficulties getting transportation, working hours, child care, or other socioeconomic circumstances. Other barriers may be related to shame or embarrassment.

Create a list of the vocabulary that would help you talk to a client about these barriers and write the English words on index cards. Look for the appropriate translation in Spanish and write it on the back of the card. Make at least twenty-five cards. Continue this collection of vocabulary whenever you encounter a new word that you would like to use with clients.

6. Actividades para divertirse
Activities for fun

Por ahora, usted entiende su proprio estilo de aprender
. . . y cómo motivarse. Para compartir su entusiasmo por aprender
y su manera de superar barreras, piense en uno o dos "dichos" o
frases para orientar a otros a continuar su aprendizaje del español.
Péquelos a la pared. Aquí hay algunos ejemplos en inglés:

*By now, you understand your own style of learning . . . and how
to motivate yourself. To share your enthusiasm for learning and your
way of overcoming barriers, think of one or two "sayings" to help
others continue learning Spanish. Hang them on the wall! Here are
some English examples:*

- *Watch out for unrealistic expectations!*

- *Give up notions of perfection and get your mouth moving!*

- *There is more to Spanish than "Quiero Taco Bell."*

- *Be a sponge—absorb what you can. Wring yourself out often
and begin again!*

- *Walk, talk, and feel Spanish!*

7. En la comunidad
In the community

La próxima vez que vaya al supermercado, visite la sección de"la comida internacional." Escoja una bebida o comida que quiera probar. Si le gustó esa bebida o comida, traiga una muestra a la próxima clase para compartir con sus compañeros.

The next time you're in the supermarket, visit the "international food" section. Choose a food or beverage that you would like to try. If you liked it, bring a sample with you to the next class to share with your classmates.

Or

Póngase en contacto con un cliente con quien ya ha hablado sobre comidas y pídale una receta fácil de sus comidas favoritas. Prepare la comida en su casa y dígale a su cliente qué tanto le gustó.

Follow up with the client with whom you talked about foods and ask for a simple recipe for one of their favorite dishes. Prepare it at home and let your client know how much you liked it.

8. Diálogo: La semana próxima: Entrevista con el consejero del abuso de sustancias
Dialogue: The next week: Interview with the substance abuse counselor

Español	English
◆ Buenos días. Yo me llamo Peter Hunt. ▶ Buenos días.	◆ *Good morning. My name is Peter Hunt.* ▶ *Good morning.*
◆ Yo trabajo con personas que quizás tengan problemas con el consumo de drogas. ¿Cómo se llama usted? ▶ Me llamo Luis Alfonso Pérez Mendoza. Llámeme Luis Pérez, señor.	◆ *I work with people who may have problems with substance abuse. What is your name?* ▶ *My name is Luis Alfonso Pérez Mendoza. Call me Luis Pérez, sir.*

Español _(continuación)_	English _(continued)_
◆ La policía le arrestó la semana pasada. ¿Me puede decir que pasó? ❱ Yo estuve en casa de mi amigo viendo un partido de fútbol. Tuve que volver a mi casa porque tenía que trabajar el día siguiente.	◆ _The police picked you up last week. Can you tell me what happened?_ ❱ _I was at my friend's house watching a soccer game. I had to go home because I had to go to work the next day._
◆ ¿Tomó bebidas alcohólicas con su amigo? ❱ Pues sí, tomamos.	◆ _Did you drink alcoholic beverages with your friend?_ ❱ _Of course we drank._
◆ ¿Qué clase de bebidas tomó? ❱ Tomé unas cervezas con mis amigos.	◆ _What kind of drinks did you have?_ ❱ _I drank some beer with my friends._
◆ ¿Por cuánto tiempo tomó? ❱ Por tres horas.	◆ _How long were you drinking?_ ❱ _For three hours._
◆ ¿Cuántas bebidas tomó? ❱ Cada uno de nosotros tomamos tres botellas de cerveza.	◆ _How many drinks did you have?_ ❱ _Each of us had three bottles of beer._
◆ ¿Usó otras sustancias como la marijuana u otras drogas? ❱ No, solamente tomamos cervezas.	◆ _Did you use any other substance, like marijuana or other drugs?_ ❱ _No, we only drank beer._
◆ ¿Usted sabe que no es legal beber y manejar? ❱ Sí, pero yo creí que si manejaba despacio nada pasaría. Pero veo que cometí un error.	◆ _Do you know that it is illegal to drink and drive?_ ❱ _Yes, but I thought that if I drove slowly, nothing would happen. I see that I made a mistake._
◆ Su licencia de manejar está suspendida por tres meses. Ahora, ¿cómo va a ir a trabajar? ❱ Puedo tomar el bus; pasa cerca de mi casa.	◆ _Your driver's license is suspended for three months. Now, how are you going to get to work?_ ❱ _I can catch the bus; it passes near my house._
◆ No va a tratar de manejar sin su licencia, ¿verdad? ❱ No, señor. No quiero más problemas con la ley.	◆ _You're not going to try to drive without your license, right?_ ❱ _No, sir. I don't want any more problems with the law._

Paso Cuatro

Conflicto en la familia:
Transiciones y temores
Conflict in the family: Transitions and fears

1. Para la reunión del grupo
For the group meeting

🔲 Antes de la reunión, escuche el diálogo "Charlando con el tutor: Transiciones en la familia" (http://unmpress.com/UserFiles/Audio/Spanish_for_Mental_Health_Professionals/Paso5.mp3) y lea la historia sobre cambios que pasan a la familia Chávez.

🙁 *Before getting together, listen to the dialogue "Chatting with the tutor: Transitions in the family" (http://unmpress.com/UserFiles/Audio/Spanish_for_Mental_Health_Professionals/Paso5.mp3) and read the story about some of the changes that are happening to the Chávez family.*

1.A. Cultura latina en contexto
Latino culture in context

"Balancing New Ways and Old in the Family"

For our family, the move to the United States has meant many harsh changes. The fear of arriving in a place where you do not understand and may not be understood . . . the fear of not making friends. All these fears are present when you face the unknown.

—*Juana*

The Chávez family is celebrating Emilia's birthday. This birthday is special. It is the first that the whole family has celebrated together in several years. Francisco Chávez, Emilia's dad, came to the United States six years ago. After being separated for almost three years, Juana and the children, Sergio and Emilia, now ten and eleven years old, crossed the Rio Grande to join their father.

The transition has been hard in many ways, especially for the children. Juana says that in the beginning the children seemed to be uncomfortable with their father. "I felt that they were treating him as a stepfather since it has been so long since they had seen him."

Now, another challenge threatens the harmony of the family. "I do not speak English very well," says Juana. "Since Francisco is always at work, I rely on our children to translate for me—at the doctor's, at the bank, and at the post office." But her reliance on the children has weakened her authority as a parent. "The children are becoming rebellious. They talk back to me when I say something. Or, they speak in English so that I can't understand. Among themselves, they hardly speak Spanish these days."

Francisco is particularly upset at the children's lack of respect for their mother. He doesn't see how the use of two languages could cause such a conflict in a family. Juana agrees with him but doesn't know how to make her kids "behave" as children do in Mexico. She worries about her "bad English," her husband's long work hours, the lack of support from her extended family, and, most of all, her children's future here in the United States.

Francisco and Juana seem to have forgotten the many changes that accompanied their move to the United States. They seem to focus instead only on their different styles of discipline. "But, I think he is too harsh. He even threatened to cancel Emilia's birthday. This time I pleaded with him not to, but I don't know what will happen next time."

1.B. Charlas para empezar la reunión
Conversations to start the meeting

⧈ Use su mejor español y su imaginación para describir lo que ve en la foto. Conteste las preguntas relacionadas con la historia con su mejor español. ¿Hay otras cosas que quiere saber? ¿Qué son?

Use your best Spanish and your imagination to describe what you see in the photograph. Answer the questions related to the story in your best Spanish. Are there other things that you want to ask? What are they?

a. ¿ Qué pasa en la foto? ¿Qué costumbres ve usted en la foto?
    What is happening in the photograph? What customs do you see in the photograph?

b. ¿ Quién está celebrando el cumpleaños con ellos?
    Who is celebrating the birthday with them?

c. ¿ Qué transiciones, cree Ud., son las más difíciles para esta familia?
    What transitions do you think are the most difficult for this family?

d. ¿ Qué sugerencias tiene usted para balancear las costumbres nuevas y viejas para Juana y Francisco?
    What suggestions do you have for balancing new ways and old for Juana and Francisco?

1.C. Practique el diálogo
Practice the dialogue

⧈ En grupos de dos, repase el diálogo que escuchó en este paso. Escoja un grupo para recitar el diálogo en clase. O, prepare otro diálogo basado en su experiencia con una familia latina.

In groups of two, review the dialogue that you listened to for this paso. Select one group to recite the dialogue for the class. Or, prepare another dialogue based on your experience with a Latino family.

2. Verbos útiles en el campo de salud mental
Useful verbs in the field of mental health

2.A. Ir + a + infinitivo
To go + to + infinitive

En inglés y en español, usted puede expresar una acción en el futuro con la estructura "ir + a + infinitivo." El cuadro da algunos ejemplos de cómo reconocer y usar la estructura en conversaciones con sus pacientes. Practique su pronunciación leyendo las frases en voz alta.

In English and Spanish, you can describe an action occurring in the future by using the "to go + to + infinitive" structure. The table gives you some examples of how to recognize and use the structure in conversations with patients. Practice your pronunciation by reading the phrases out loud.

Español	English
◆ Ir a pedir ayuda a la clínica ▶ Voy a pedir ayuda. ▶ Mi hermana y yo vamos a pedir ayuda a la clínica.	◆ *Going to ask for help from the clinic* ▶ *I am going to ask for help.* ▶ *My sister and I are going to ask for help at the clinic.*
◆ Ir a decirle lo que pasó ▶ El padre va a decirle lo que pasó. ▶ Ellos van a decirle lo que pasó.	◆ *Going to tell you what happened* ▶ *The priest is going to tell you what happened.* ▶ *They are going to tell you what happened.*
◆ Ir a comprar un pastel ▶ La mamá va a comprar un pastel. ▶ Yo voy a comprar el pastel.	◆ *Going to buy a cake* ▶ *The mother is going to buy a cake.* ▶ *I am going to buy a cake.*
◆ Ir a pagar ▶ Voy a pagar en efectivo. ▶ Usted no va a pagar "con cash."	◆ *Going to pay* ▶ *I am going to pay in cash.* ▶ *You are not going to pay cash.*

2.B. "Conocer" o "saber"
To know "someone" or "something"

Hay dos verbos que indican "to know" en español. "Conocer" significa "to know someone" o "to meet someone" por la primera vez. Se usa también "conocer" para indicar familiaridad. Por ejemplo: "No conozco la ciudad de Santiago." "Saber" significa "to know something," tales como el día o la fecha. Por ejemplo: "Yo sé que hoy es miércoles."

There are two verbs in Spanish that indicate "to know." "Conocer" means to know someone or to meet someone for the first time. One can also use "conocer" to indicate familiarity. For example: "I don't know the city of Santiago," that is, I have never been there. "Saber"* means to know something, such as the day or date. For example: "I know that today is Wednesday." (*The preterit of "saber" is irregular: supe, supiste, supo, supimos, supieron.)

Yo _conozco_ a la familia Gómez.	*I know the Gomez family.*
Van a _conocer_ a su maestra de ESL mañana.	*They are going to meet their ESL teacher tomorrow.*
Yo _sé_ la fecha de la clase.	*I know the date of the class.*
Ellos _sabían_ las respuestas.	*They knew the answers.*

Práctica A
Reorganize the letters below to form words taken from the story about Emilia's birthday. Maybe you will need a dictionary. It's difficult! (Hint: here are the English translations [not in order] of the unscrambled words [birthday, celebrate, hardly, harmony, harsh, rebellious, respect, together, translate, work]).

Palabras mezcladas	Palabras correctas	Palabras mezcladas	Palabras correctas
tadrricu	_____	nomraaí	_____
aeasnp	_____	unsotj	_____
otsrpee	_____	lrcareeb	_____
reveos	_____	trrjbaaa	_____
cmlaoupeñs	_____	beeedlr	_____

Práctica B

Complete the story about the ESL teacher's meeting with Juana's children. Choose the correct verb for "to know" or "to meet." You also need to choose the tense and number for each of the missing verbs.

"La visita para conocer a la maestra de ESL"

La semana pasada, la maestra de ESL _____ (conocer o saber) a los

niños de Juana. Después de _____ (conocer o saber) a la señorita

Clifford, los chicos _____ (hablar) con ella sobre las cosas nuevas en

los EE.UU. Su mamá _____ (mostrar) interés en lo que la maestra

decía. La mamá _____ (estar o ser) preocupada por los niños.

La mamá _____ (querer) llevarlos a un psicólogo, pero la señorita

Clifford ofreció charlar con ellos." Yo_____ (tener) muchos temores

por los cambios," dijo la señorita. Durante la visita, la mamá _____

(conocer o saber) que ella tiene que escuchar—sin interrumpir. La señorita

Clifford, después de charlar con los niños, comentó que ellos ya _____

(conocer o saber) bien muchas de las cosas de la cultura nueva. "Ellos

_____ (ir) a adaptarse bien," aseguró la maestra. "Gracias por su

visita. Es un gusto _____ los," (conocer o saber) dijo ella a los

chicos. "Gracias," _____ (contestar) Emilia y Sergio en coro.

Práctica C

Pretend that you work in a community mental health clinic. Take turns role-playing an interaction between a patient and a provider. The patient begins with a complaint. The provider's first task is to assess if the presenting complaint is the patient's key concern—or if something else is really the concern. Ask about symptoms, duration, and severity. After a reasonable number of questions, stop. Tell your probable diagnosis if you are the provider. Ask the patient to confirm the diagnosis or tell the "real" problem. Use as much Spanish as you can; use some "Spanglish," if necessary. Notice how language is carried in context, even if some English is used.

3. Palabras y expresiones nuevas
New words and expressions

3.A. Algunos verbos relacionados con el abuso
Some verbs related to abuse

Abajo hay una lista de verbos que indican una acción de abuso o violencia. Su cliente puede usar estas palabras para describir una situación en la que hubo/pudo haber sido un incidente de violencia doméstica. Léalas y ponga cada una en una frase para practicar.

Below is a list of verbs that indicate abuse or violence. Your client may use these words to describe a situation in which there was/may have been an incident of domestic violence. Read them and put each one in a sentence for practice.

Español	*English*	Español	*English*
abofetear, cachetear	*to slap*	aislar	*to isolate*
ahorcar, estrangular	*to choke*	apretar	*to press, to hold down*
amenazar	*to threaten*	aventar, tirar	*to throw*
burlar	*to make fun of*	controlar	*to control*
empujar	*to push*	destruir	*to destroy*
forzar	*to force*	estirar, jalar	*to pull*
gritar	*to yell*	golpear	*to batter*
humillar	*to embarrass*	herir	*to wound, to hurt*
insultar	*to insult*	ignorar	*to ignore, to neglect*
minimizar, ridiculizar	*to belittle*	matar	*to kill*
patear	*to kick*	morder	*to bite*
prohibir	*to prohibit*	pegar	*to hit*

Práctica D

This paso introduces new verbs that you may hear a client using. You should know them all. Below are seven verbs from the list. Write questions that you could use to ask your client about his or her situation. Be both firm and sensitive. Read the sentences aloud to get feedback on your choice of words.

Verbos *Verbs*	Preguntas *Questions*
burlar *to make fun of*	¿Su pareja se burlaba de usted *Did your partner make fun of you?*
cachetear *to slap*	
empujar *to push*	
golpear *to batter*	
gritar *to yell*	
insultar *to insult*	
prohibir *to prohibit*	

Práctica E

When you are interviewing or talking with a client for the first time, there are many details that you want to ask about. You may want to ask about the decision to migrate, the migration journey itself, settling into a new home, family stress, enrolling the children in school, learning to drive, or finding familiar foods. Pick a topic area of particular interest. Generate a list of questions; underline the English words that you do not know in Spanish. Write the English words on index cards. Look up the translations in Spanish. Continue adding to this list as you explore new topics with your clients.

3.B. Partes del cuerpo
Parts of the body

Abajo hay una lista de vocabulario del cuerpo humano que su cliente puede usar cuando describe síntomas. Aprenda estas palabras y cómo usarlas.

Below is a list of vocabulary for body parts that your client may use to describe symptoms. Learn these words and how to use them.

Español	English	Español	English
La Cabeza	*The Head*	**El Cuerpo**	*The Body*
La Cara	*Face*	**El Torso**	*Trunk*
el cabello/el pelo	*hair*	el hombro	*shoulder*
la frente	*forehead*	el pecho	*chest*
la mejilla/el cachete	*cheek*	la espalda	*back*
el mentón	*chin*	la cintura	*waist*
la mandíbula	*jaw*	el abdomen	*abdomen*
la oreja/el oído	*ear (outer/inner)*	la cadera	*hip*
la barba	*beard*	las nalgas	*buttocks*
el bigote	*moustache*		
El Ojo	*Eye*	**El Brazo**	*Arm*
las cejas	*eyebrows*	la axila/el sobaco	*armpit*
las pestañas	*eyelashes*	el antebrazo	*forearm*
el párpado	*eyelid*	el codo	*elbow*
el iris	*iris*	la muñeca	*wrist*
la pupila	*pupil*	la mano	*hand*
		el nudillo	*knuckle*
		el dedo	*finger*
La Nariz	*Nose*	**La Pierna**	*Leg*
el orificio nasal	*nostril*	el muslo	*thigh*
		la rodilla	*knee*
La Boca	*Mouth*	la pantorrilla	*calf*
el labio	*lip*	el pie	*foot*
el diente	*tooth*	el tobillo	*ankle*
la lengua	*tongue*	el talón	*heel*
El Cuello	*Neck*	el dedo del pie	*toe*

3.C. Nombres de familias latinos
Latino family names

In Latin America, more than one last name is used to describe family relationships. Latino names consist of a first and middle name, or "given names," followed by the father's last name, followed by the mother's paternal surname—in that order. Many people shorten a name by using only an initial for the maternal surname. For example, in the story, Francisco's name would be written Juan Francisco Gómez Calderón or Francisco Gómez C. The surname by which official records are kept is the first surname!

It is important for Americans and Latinos to understand these differences, in order to consistently record the correct surname on health records. Among Latinos, the first last name is the equivalent of a last name in the United States.

Write your name, Latino style, below. Use this model in the clinic.

Write your father's name on the lines below:

father's given name/slast name	*father's father's last name*	*father's mother's maiden name*

Write your mother's name on the lines below:

mother's given name/s	*mother's father's last name*	*mother's mother's maiden name*

Write your name here:

your given name/s	*your last name (from your father)*	*your mother's maiden name*

Write your name, Latino style, using your principal surname and an initial:

_____

Práctica F

Draw an outline of a human figure on a large sheet of paper. Write the name of all the parts of the body that you can remember on the figure, in the correct position. Hang the paper on the back of the door of your office and review the new vocabulary every day until you remember it all. To make this exercise livelier, divide the group into two teams. Give each group large sheets of paper. Tell each group to trace an outline of someone's body. Then, write as many body part names as they can. Give the group ten or fifteen minutes to complete the task. Give the winning team a prize!

Práctica G

In your best Spanish, or Spanglish, write a paragraph about the problem of domestic violence—as a reaction to the stress of the migration transition. Reflect on ways in which similar problems are handled in sending countries. Also, give some attention in your paragraph to barriers to seeking health care here in the United States.

Hang your paragraphs on the wall. Take ten minutes to read each other's commentaries. Then, hold a discussion about the group's perception. Finally, suggest some ways in which individuals and organizations could act to reduce barriers for those seeking care.

Práctica H

To practice the names of the parts of the body (or another focused vocabulary), write the letters of each word on 1 × 1 inch cut-out squares of card stock. Add a few additional vowel cards, as well as a couple of ll's, rr's, and ñ's. Shuffle the cards, then turn them blank side up. Each player draws ten cards; the first player may write any word to get the game in play. The next player also tries to create a word from the focused vocabulary, or another word. Each card played is worth two points if the player creates a word from the focused vocabulary; other words are worth only one point per card played. Practice translations; keep score; have fun!

4. Instrumento de evaluación: Preguntas relacionadas con la violencia doméstica
Assessment tool: Questions related to domestic violence

Español	English
¿Hay alguien que intenta controlar lo que hace usted o, a quién usted ve o habla? ¿Quién es?	Does someone try to control what you do or who you see or talk to? Who is it?
¿Hay alguien que le dice cosas feas o dañinas? ¿Quién es? ¿Cómo se llama?	Does someone say mean or hurtful things to you? Who is it? What is this person's name?
¿Le tiene miedo a su pareja o su novio cuando él se pone enojado?	Are you afraid of your husband or your boyfriend when he gets angry?
¿Ha amenazado de matarla o herirla?	Has this person ever threatened to kill or injure you?
¿Su pareja la ha . . . empujado? golpeado? pateado? sofocado?	Has your husband or boyfriend . . . pushed you? hit you? kicked you? choked you?
¿Tiene miedo de que su pareja vaya a lastimar a sus niños?	Are you afraid that your partner will injure your children?
¿Le ha hablado a alguien acerca de este comportamiento? ¿Ha pedido ayuda a alguien?	Have you told anyone about this behavior? Have you asked anyone for help?
¿Se siente segura en casa? ¿Necesita un lugar seguro para quedarse por unos días?	Do you feel safe at home? Do you need a place to stay for a few days?

5. Durante la semana que viene
During the coming week

[icon] Dibuje su árbol genealógico (o el árbol genealógico de uno de sus clientes) en español, incluyendo el nombre de la persona y su relación con usted (o su cliente).

No se olvide de la lista de palabras de la familia del paso dos si necesita ayuda con el vocabulario.

[icon] *Draw your family tree (or what you know of the family tree of one of your patients) in Spanish, including both the name of the person and their relation to you (or your patient).*

Don't forget the list of family words that you have in paso 2 if you need help with the vocabulary.

Or

[icon] Vaya a la biblioteca pública para buscar libros de cuentos en español que usted ya conoce en inglés. Saque uno o dos. Mientras que está leyendo, note cómo se cuenta la historia en español. ¿Hay palabras nuevas que usted puede comprender por el contexto?

[icon] *Go to a local public library to look for Spanish language children's storybooks that are familiar to you in English. Check out one or two. As you read them, notice how the story is told in Spanish. Are there new words that you can understand because of the context?*

6. Actividades para divertirse
Activities for fun

Trate de cocinar algunas de estas recetas. Lea la receta primero en español y después verifíquela en inglés. ¡Buen provecho!

Try to cook some of these recipes. Read the recipe in Spanish first and only afterward check the recipe in English. ¡Buen provecho!

MARINERA (Paraguaya)	*MARINERA (Paraguayan)*
2 tazas de harina	*2 cups of flour*
4 carnes cortadas de bistec	*4 slices of beef*
2 huevos	*2 eggs*
$^1/_2$ taza de agua	*$^1/_2$ cup of water*
2 dientes de ajo, picados	*2 cloves of garlic, minced*
2 tazas de aceite de oliva	*2 cups of olive oil*
Sal y pimienta al gusto	*Salt and pepper to taste*

En un tazón, bata la harina con el agua y los huevos. Bata hasta que se forme una mezcla moldeable agregando más agua si está muy densa. Cuando los ingredientes estén bien mezclados, agregue los ajos, sal, y pimienta. En una sartén, caliente el aceite de oliva. Tome el bistec y póngalo en la mezcla. Fría la carne en la sartén. Cocine hasta que ambos lados estén dorados. Sirva la marinera con su ensalada favorita. Para dos personas.

In a bowl, mix the flour with the water and the eggs. Mix until a batter is formed, adding more water if the mixture is too thick. When the ingredients are mixed, add the garlic, salt, and pepper. In a pan, heat the olive oil. Take the beef and coat in batter. Fry the beef in the pan. Cook until both sides turn golden. Serve the marinera with your favorite salad. Serves two people.

PICADILLO *(ground beef with apples, olives, and almonds)*

3 cucharadas de aceite de oliva	*3 tablespoons olive oil*
2 libras de carne molida	*2 pounds ground beef*
1 taza de cebolla picada	*1 cup chopped onions*
$^1/_4$ cucharadita de ajo picado	*$^1/_4$ teaspoon chopped garlic*
1 taza de tomates enlatado, picados, y secos	*1 cup canned tomatoes, chopped, drained*
2 manzanas, peladas y cortadas	*2 apples, peeled and chopped*
3 jalapeños chiles enlatados, secos, sin semillas, y cortados en redondas	*3 canned jalapeño chiles, drained, seeded, and cut into rounds*
$^1/_2$ taza de pasas sin semillas	*$^1/_2$ cup seedless raisins*
10 aceitunas con pimiento cortadas a la mitad	*10 pimiento-stuffed green olives, cut in half*
$^1/_8$ cucharadita de canela y clavos molidos	*$^1/_8$ teaspoon ground cinnamon and cloves*
1 cucharadita de sal	*1 teaspoon salt*
$^1/_2$ cucharadita de pimiento negro	*$^1/_2$ teaspoon black pepper*
$^1/_2$ taza de almendras picadas	*$^1/_2$ cup slivered almonds*

En una sartén, caliente 2 cucharadas de aceite de oliva hasta que esté bien caliente. Agregue la carne molida y cocínela, mezclando constantemente. Cuando la carne esté cocinada, agregue la cebolla y el ajo. Baje el fuego y cocine por 4 o 5 minutos antes de añadir los tomates, las manzanas, los chiles, las pasas, aceitunas, canela y clavos, sal, y pimienta. Cocine a fuego lento por 20 minutos, mezclando de vez en cuando.

En otra sartén, caliente la otra cucharada de aceite de oliva. Cocine las almendras por 2 o 3 minutos, hasta que estén doradas. Luego, mézclelas con el picadillo justo antes de servirlo. El picadillo puede ser servido como una entrada, acompañado de arroz o frijoles. Receta para 4 a 6 personas.

In a skillet, heat 2 tablespoons of the olive oil until hot. Add the ground beef and cook it, stirring constantly. When the beef is browned, stir in the onions and garlic. Reduce the heat and cook for 4 or 5 minutes before adding the tomatoes, apples, chiles, raisins, green olives, cinnamon, cloves, salt, and pepper. Simmer over low heat for 20 minutes, stirring occasionally.

In a small skillet heat the remaining 1 tablespoon of oil. Brown the almonds for 2 or 3 minutes, until they are golden brown. Then, stir them into the picadillo just before serving it. Picadillo may be served as a main-dish course, accompanied by rice or beans. Serves 4 to 6 people.

GALLETAS DE TROCITOS DE CHOCOLATE   *CHOCOLATE CHIP COOKIES*

1 taza de mantequilla blanda o manteca	*1 cup softened butter or shortening*
2 huevos	*2 eggs*
1 taza de azúcar	*1 cup granulated sugar*
$^1/_2$ taza de azúcar morena	*$^1/_2$ cup firmly packed brown sugar*
2 cucharaditas de vainilla	*2 teaspoons vanilla*
$2^1/_2$ tazas de harina cernida	*$2^1/_2$ cups sifted flour*
1 cucharadita de bicarbonato	*1 teaspoon bicarbonate of soda*
1 cucharadita de sal	*1 teaspoon salt*
1 taza de nueces picadas	*1 cup chopped nuts*
12 onzas de trocitos de chocolate	*12 ounces of chocolate chips*

Bata la mantequilla, los huevos, el azúcar, el azúcar morena, y la vainilla hasta que la mezcla esté esponjosa. Agregue los ingredientes secos y mezcle bien. Agregue la sal, las nueces, y los trocitos de chocolate. Vierta por cucharillas sobre el papel de hornear engrasado separadas en 6 centímetros de distancia. Hornee a 375°–400° por 8 a 10 minutos. Rinde 6 docenas.

Beat butter, eggs, sugar, brown sugar, and vanilla until fluffy. Add dry ingredients; blend well. Stir in nuts and pieces of chocolate. Drop from teaspoon onto greased baking sheets, 2 inches apart. Bake in moderate oven (375°–400°) for 8 to 10 minutes. Makes 6 dozen.

7. En la comunidad
In the community

Vaya a una escuela, una organización comunitaria, un hospital, o una clínica de salud mental para entrevistar a un representante acerca de los tipos de servicios de salud mental que ofrecen en español. También, pregunte a los representantes si ellos encuentran puntos débiles con estos servicios y acerca de otras intervenciones que desearían ver añadidas a los servicios existentes.

Go to a school, a community organization, a hospital, or a mental health clinic and interview a representative there about the kinds of mental health services that they offer in Spanish. Also, ask the representative if they are aware of limitations of these services and about other interventions they would like to see added to existing services. Or

Entreviste a un cliente o a un amigo latino acerca de actividades que le ayudaría a acostumbrarse a la vida en los Estados Unidos y que le gustaría ver que fueran ofrecidas. También, pregúntele qué lugares son más apropiados para estas actividades.

Interview a Latino client or friend about activities they would like to see offered that would help them adjust to life in the United States. Also, ask them what are the most appropriate places for these activities.

8. Diálogo: Charlando con el tutor: Transiciones en la familia

Dialogue: Chatting with the tutor: Transitions in the family

Español	English
◆ Hola, Juana. ¿Cómo está? ▶ No muy bien, Mary.	◆ *Hello, Juana. How are you?* ▶ *Not well, Mary.*
◆ Espero que no esté molesta porque le dí mucha tarea la semana pasada. ▶ No, Mary. Las tareas son muy interesantes. Además me ayuda bastante para aprender el inglés.	◆ *I hope you are not upset because I gave you a lot of homework last week.* ▶ *No, Mary. The homework is very interesting. Also, it helps me a lot to learn English.*
◆ Entonces, ¿por qué está tan triste? ▶ Hay mucha tensión en mi casa entre Francisco y los niños.	◆ *Then, why are you so sad?* ▶ *There is a lot of tension at home between Francisco and the kids.*
◆ Y, ¿por qué? ▶ Los niños están volviéndose muy rebeldes. No obedecen y no quieren hablar español.	◆ *And why?* ▶ *The kids are becoming very rebellious. They do not obey and do not want to speak in Spanish.*
◆ Debe ser muy difícil para los niños trasladarse a un lugar nuevo. ▶ Sí, pero Francisco dice que los niños necesitan más disciplina.	◆ *It must be difficult for the children to move to a new place.* ▶ *Yes, but Francisco says that the kids need more discipline.*
◆ Juana, usted no parece estar de acuerdo con él. ▶ No, porque yo creo que los niños están pasando por un período de adaptación.	◆ *Juana, you do not seem to agree with him.* ▶ *No, because I think the kids are going through a period of transition.*
◆ ¿Le habló usted a Francisco acerca de lo que usted piensa? ▶ Sí, pero Francisco piensa que yo soy muy flexible con ellos. Yo creo que es él quién está pasando de la raya.	◆ *Did you talk to Francisco about what you think?* ▶ *Yes, but Francisco thinks that I am too flexible with them. I think he is the one who is crossing the line.*
◆ ¿Por qué dice que él está pasando de la raya—o ha pasado el límite—como dice alguna gente? ▶ El otro día, Francisco amenazó en cancelar el cumpleaños de Emilia.	◆ *Why do you think he is crossing the line—or has crossed the limit—as some people say?* ▶ *The other day, he threatened to cancel Emilia's birthday.*

Español *(continuación)*	English *(continued)*
◆ Y, ¿cómo la tomó Emilia?	◆ *And, how did she take it?*
▶ Emilia no paraba de llorar. Yo tuve que intervenir. Gracias a Dios que él accedió a no cancelar la fiesta.	▶ *Emilia did not stop crying. I had to intervene. Thankfully, he agreed not to cancel the party.*
◆ Parece que al final Francisco la escucha a usted.	◆ *It looks like in the end Francisco listened to you.*
▶ Al principio, sí. Pero ahora, ya no. Ultimamente él ha estado muy estresado por el trabajo.	▶ *He did in the beginning. But he doesn't anymore. Lately he has been under a lot of stress because of his work.*
◆ ¿Pero yo creí que a Francisco le gustaba su trabajo?	◆ *But I thought he liked his job?*
▶ Sí, le gusta mucho. Pero le cortaron las horas porque dice que la fábrica no va bien.	▶ *Yes, he likes it a lot. But they cut his work hours because the factory is not doing well.*
◆ Entiendo, debe de ser muy duro para Francisco y los niños. Yo viví en Bolivia antes de ser maestra de ESL. Y recuerdo que es muy difícil de adaptarse a un lugar nuevo.	◆ *I understand. It must be difficult for Francisco and the kids. I lived in Bolivia before becoming an ESL teacher. And I remember how difficult it is to live in a new place.*
▶ Me gustaría que alguien como usted hablara con ellos.	▶ *I would like for someone like you to talk with them.*
◆ Juana, si usted quiere, yo puedo reunirme con toda la familia un día y hablar con ellos.	◆ *Juana, if you want, I could meet with the whole family one day and talk with them.*
▶ Eso sería muy bueno porque usted entiende las dos culturas, la latina y la americana.	▶ *That would be great since you understand the two cultures, Latin American and American.*
◆ Ahora que charlamos acerca de su problema, volvamos a la lección.	◆ *Now that we have talked about your problem, let's get to the lesson.*
▶ Sí, Mary. Gracias por su ayuda.	▶ *Yes, Mary. Thank you for your help.*

Paso Seis

Creando puentes entre culturas
Building bridges across cultures

1. Para la reunión del grupo
For the group meeting

![icon] Antes de la reunión, escuche el diálogo "Apoyo social de la comunidad" (http://unmpress.com/UserFiles/Audio/Spanish_ for_Mental_Health_Professionals/Paso6.mp3) y lea la historia de Josefina sobre el apoyo que le ha ofrecido la iglesia y las agencias comunitarias.

![icon] *Before getting together, listen to the dialogue "Social support in the community" (http://unmpress.com/UserFiles/Audio/Spanish_for_ Mental_Health_Professionals/Paso6.mp3) and read Josefina's story about the support offered her by the church and other community agencies.*

1.A. Cultura latina en contexto
Latino culture in context

"Josefina's Bridge to the Future"

We are in a program at the Centro Latino nearby. There are more than twenty of us in total. We never feel alone.

—Josefina

When families migrate to the United States, they attempt to recreate elements of the culture they left behind. Latino families often live close to one another and join local churches and community centers. Through these neighborhood connections, families can maintain the continuity of faces, voices, smells . . . and language.

Josefina emigrated from El Salvador. She finds that the church's support has eased her family's transition. "We are grateful we found this church. People are nice. The church allows families to take the Virgin of Guadalupe home for a week just like we did at home. It is such an honor to take the Virgin home."

Community organizations also play a pivotal role in providing support. Even though many members of her extended family crossed the border and live nearby, Josefina still feels confused at times. She recently joined the *club de mujeres* at a local community center; several American women who speak Spanish well lead the group. She feels the support group has helped explain many of the new, sometimes strange, things around her. "We get together with other women once a week. We learn some English; we talk about our kids, their schools, and things we can do with our families on the weekends. Meeting like this helps me to feel less confused."

Community activities such as these provide not only emotional support but also skills to help Latina immigrants overcome challenges faced in the United States. As an ESL (English as a Second Language) student at the community center, Josefina feels that the class has taught her not only language skills but also given her new confidence. "I feel more certain going out and doing things by myself. Now, I do not depend so much on my husband and my kids. Everybody is happier."

Josefina attributes her smooth transition to this new country to the programs organized by the church and community centers. "These programs are so important because they make me feel that I am not the only person faced with challenges in this country. It makes me realize that there are other women working hard to adjust to new ways—just like my family is doing."

1.B. Charlas para empezar la reunión
Conversations to start the meeting

⬛ Use su mejor español y su imaginación para describir lo que ve en la foto. Responda a las preguntas relacionadas con la historia con su mejor español. ¿Hay otras cosas que le gustaría preguntar? ¿Qué son?

☺ *Use your best Spanish and your imagination to describe what you see in the photograph. Answer the questions related to the story in Spanish or English. Are there other things that you want to ask? What are they?*

a. ¿Cómo cree usted que se siente la familia en la foto?
    How do you think the family in the photograph feels?

b. En la historia, ¿por qué es importante llevar a la Virgen a la casa?
    In the story, why is it important to take the Virgin home?

c. ¿Por qué razones Josefina va al club de mujeres?
    What are some reasons that Josefina goes to the women's club?

d. ¿Qué cosas ayudan a Josefina y su familia a acostumbrarse mejor a los Estados Unidos? ¿Qué sugerencias tiene Ud.?
    What things help Josefina and her family adjust better to the United States? What suggestions do you have?

1.C. Practique el diálogo
Practice the dialogue

⬛ En grupos de dos, repase el diálogo que escuchó en este paso. Escoja dos estudiantes para recitar el diálogo (use notas si las necesita) en frente del grupo. Escoja otro par para presentar una variación del diálogo basada en sus experiencias de trabajo.

☺ *In groups of two, review the dialogue that you listened to for this paso. Select two students to recite the dialogue (use notes if necessary) in front of the group. Select another pair to present a variation of the dialogue based on their work experiences.*

2. Verbos útiles en el campo de salud mental
Useful verbs in the field of mental health

2.A. El verbo "gustar"
The verb "to like"

"Gustar" es un verbo importantísimo en español. Aunque se puede traducir fácilmente como "to like" en inglés, es, literalmente, "to be pleasing to" cuando se usa la palabra en español. Cuando se usa este verbo en español, la frase parece estar escrita al revés. Hay dos formas del verbo en el presente: "gusta" y "gustan." Observe los ejemplos:

"To like" is a very important verb in Spanish. What translates loosely as "to like" in English is, literally, "to be pleasing to" when the word is used in Spanish. When this verb is used in Spanish, it seems that the sentence is written backward. In general, only two forms of the verb are used: "gusta" and "gustan." Observe the models:

(A mí), me gusta la clínica.

> *Translation: I like the clinic.*
> *Literal translation: The clinic pleases me.*

(A mí), me gustan los doctores.

> *Translation: I like the doctors.*
> *Literal translation: The doctors please me.*

En la primera frase, "la clínica" es singular. Por eso, se usa la forma "gusta." En la segunda frase, "los doctores" es plural y se usa "gustan." "A mí" puede ser usado para dar énfasis, pero es opcional.

In the first sentence, "the clinic" is singular. As a result, the form "gusta" is used. In the second sentence, "the doctors" is plural and "gustan" is used. "A mí" can be used for emphasis, but it is optional.

Práctica A

Complete the sentences with the correct form of the verb "to like." Translate each sentence to English.

1. (A mí), me _____ ir a la iglesia.   _____

2. (A ella), le _____ estudiar inglés.   _____

3. (A José), no le _____ tomar agua.   _____

4. (A los chicos), les _____ los juguetes   _____

5. (A Rosa) le _____ comer pastel.   _____

6. (A los amigos) les _____ estar juntos.   _____

Práctica B

To practice the use of "gustar" a little more, have a conversation with a colleague. What aspects of your work do you like the most? Which aspects don't you like much? What do you like to do after work? On the weekends? Talk about different situations using both the singular and plural forms of the verb "to like."

Práctica C

Circle the Spanish words in this word puzzle. There are fourteen words (across and down); each one appears in the story for this paso. Some may be new vocabulary. Practice the new words; make flash cards to help increase your vocabulary.

A	I	S	L	A	D	O	E	R	J	L	M
K	T	V	A	Z	C	U	L	T	U	R	A
D	E	S	P	O	S	O	E	Y	R	Y	T
L	S	U	E	L	T	O	M	X	E	T	R
U	T	P	L	H	I	B	E	C	Z	E	Á
C	A	S	V	E	C	I	N	D	A	D	S
H	R	C	F	J	G	O	T	F	R	A	Z
A	P	O	Y	O	D	R	O	P	L	D	M
R	Q	A	U	T	O	E	S	T	I	M	A
U	Y	S	U	P	E	R	A	R	Q	V	X

2.B. Formando mandatos
Forming commands

▧◩ A veces, los profesionales de salud mental tienen que dar instrucciones a sus pacientes. En estas situaciones, usamos la forma del verbo llamado "el mandato." Formas diferentes del verbo son usados con "tú" o "usted." Pueden ser afirmativos o negativos. El cuadro presenta mandatos comunes en la práctica de salud mental. Puede usar el mandato solo o en una frase más larga.

☺ *At times, mental health professionals have to give instructions to their patients. In these situations, the form of the verb called the imperative is used. There are different forms used with "tú" or "usted." Commands can be affirmative or negative. The table lists common commands in mental health settings. You can use the command by itself or put it in a longer sentence.*

Español		English
Mandatos afirmativos		*Affirmative commands*
Tú *(with children)*	**Usted** *(with adults)*	
◆ Siéntate aquí, por favor.	◆ Siéntese aquí, por favor.	◆ *Sit here, please.*
◆ Toma esta pastilla.	◆ Tome esta pastilla.	◆ *Take this pill.*
◆ Hazlo hoy.	◆ Hágalo hoy.	◆ *Do it today.*
◆ Hablamos ahora.	◆ Hablemos ahora.	◆ *Let's talk now.*
◆ Dime toda la verdad.	◆ Dígame toda la verdad.	◆ *Tell me the truth.*
◆ Pon tu mochila aquí.	◆ Ponga su bolsa aquí.	◆ *Put your backpack (purse) here.*
◆ Pórtate bien.	—	◆ *Behave yourself.*
Mandatos negativos		*Negative commands*
◆ No lo hagas.	◆ No lo haga.	◆ *Don't do it.*
◆ No me mientas.	◆ No me mienta.	◆ *Don't lie to me.*

2.C. Expresando obligaciones
Expressing obligations

Usted puede usar también expresiones como "tener + que + infinitivo" y "hay + que + infinitivo" para indicar obligaciones. A continuación se explican las diferencias claves entre las dos expresiones.

You can also use two other structures, "tener + que + infinitive" and "hay + que + infinitive," to indicate obligations—something that one must do. The key differences between the two structures are explained below.

Tener + que + infinitivo	Used when the subject is a specific person or persons:
	
	• Mi hijo tiene que hacer la tarea todas las noches. ¡Es mucho!
	  My son has to do homework every night. It's a lot!
	
	• Usted tiene que tomarse estas pastillas.
	  You have to take these pills.
	
	• Tienen que practicar su inglés para mejorar.
	  You (plural) have to practice your English to improve.

Hay + que + infinitivo	Used when the subject is impersonal, that is, when not referring to anything or anyone in particular:
	
	• Hay que comer una dieta balanceada para mantenerse saludable.
	  You have to eat a balanced diet to stay healthy.
	
	• Hay que hacer algo divertido cada rato. No se puede trabajar todo el tiempo.
	  You have to do something fun every so often. One can't work all the time.

3. Palabras y expresiones nuevas
New words and expressions

3.A. Lugares y servicios en la comunidad
Places and services in the community

🔳 Abajo hay una lista de instituciones públicas y tipos de servicios comunitarios. Aprender estas palabras le ayudará a identificar lugares dónde su cliente puede recibir apoyo local.

🙂 *Below is a list of public institutions and types of services in your community. Learning these words will help you identify places where your client can receive local support.*

Español	English
centro de salud comunitario	*community health center*
centro latino	*Latino center*
línea de crisis, las 24 horas	*24-hour crisis center*
servicios de refugio	*shelter*
clase de inglés como segunda lengua	*English as a second language (ESL) class*
departamento de servicios sociales	*department of social services*
grupo de apoyo para mujeres abusadas (golpeadas)	*support group for battered women*
representación o abogacía	*representation or advocacy*
consejería individual	*individual counseling*
escuela	*school*
hospital, clínica, o centro de salud mental	*hospital, clinic, or mental health center*
iglesia, templo	*church, temple*
el correo	*post office*
banco	*bank*
centro commercial	*shopping center*
lavandería	*laundry*
tienda de comestibles, supermercado	*grocery store*

3.B. Ampliando su vocabulario: Preguntas "tag"
Expanding your vocabulary: "Tag" questions

🔁 A veces, charlar con su cliente puede ser "one-sided," es decir, el profesional habla y el cliente cabecea para decir "sí" o "no." Usted puede combinar una oración con una pregunta "tag" para cambiar la oración a una pregunta. En el cuadro, presentamos algunos ejemplos.

☺ *At times, chatting with a client can be "one-sided," that is to say that the professional talks and the client nods to say "yes" or "no." You can combine a statement with a "tag" question to transform a sentence into question. The table contains some examples.*

Preguntas "tag" en español	Tag questions in English
◆ María es muy timida, ¿no?	◆ *Mary is very timid, isn't she?*
◆ Usted abusaba alcohol, ¿no es cierto?	◆ *You were abusing alcohol, weren't you?*
◆ Está muy lindo afuera, ¿verdad?	◆ *It's very pretty outside, isn't it?*
◆ Su niño tiene Medicaid, ¿cierto?	◆ *Your son has Medicaid, right?*
◆ Tiene su cita el miércoles, ¿no es verdad?	◆ *Your appointment is on Wednesday, isn't it?*
◆ Quiero preguntarle algo, ¿está bien?	◆ *I'd like to ask you something, is that OK?*

Práctica D
Write other "tag questions" using the words given in the sentences you write.

centros comunitarios; ayudar: _____

niños; hablar: _____

cervezas; tomar: _____

partido de fútbol; mirar: _____

dinero; gastar: _____

inglés; hablar: _____

3.C. Otras formas de pedidos: "Favor de"
Other forms of request: "Please . . ."

⌗ Una manera más gentil de hacer un pedido es usar la expresión "favor de + infinitivo." Esta manera de hacer un pedido se usa cuando uno quiere animar a alguien a hacer algo que no sea una obligación.

☺ *A gentler way to make a request is to use the expression "favor de + infinitive." This way of making a request is used when one wants to encourage someone to do something, but something that may not be required.*

Práctica E
Put the following expressions into sentences using "tener que," "hay que," or "favor de." Explain to the group the reason you chose the expression you did.

1. tomarse estas pastillas

2. rezar con la familia

3. volver la semana entrante

4. aprender inglés

5. descansar ocho horas por la noche

6. comer una dieta balanceada

7. leer con sus niños en la tarde

8. llevar este libro a la maestra de ESL

Práctica F
In paso 2, some expressions using greetings and closings or "good-byes" were introduced. Review the closings or good-byes now. Talk about when you would use each expression. Form pairs and create a role-play about the end of a conversation or meeting between a patient and a counselor or other mental health worker. Give examples using both formal and informal conversation.

Práctica G
On the weekend, when you go out to do errands or for a ride around town, take a pad of paper and pencil with you. Write the names of community resources on the pad. Collect twenty different places: places to go for help, places to have fun. When you get home, look up the Spanish words for those you do not know. Put the new words on file cards; practice putting them in sentences. Recommend some of these settings to a client at your next meeting.

4. Instrumento de evaluación: Descubriendo las preocupaciones ocultas de Juan Pablo
Assessment tool: Uncovering Juan Pablo's hidden worries

Hola, Marta. ¿Cómo está?	*Hi, Marta. How are you?*
Estoy bien. ¿Cómo está Ud., Josefina?	*I'm good. How are you, Josefina?*
Pues, más o menos. ¿Puedo hacerle una pregunta? Ud. es una enfermera y trabaja con latinos en nuestra iglesia. Creo que podría ayudarme, Marta.	*Not so well. Could I ask you a question? You are a nurse and work with Latinos at our church. I think you might be able to help me, Marta.*
Pues, sí. Trataré de ayudarle. ¿Qué pasa?	*Well, yes, I'll try to help you. What is it?*
Pues, Marta, aunque estoy aquí por casi once años, a veces, me siento tan confundida como el día que llegué.	*Well, even though I've been here for almost eleven years, at times, I still feel as confused as the day I arrived.*
¿Puede decirme más, Josefina?	*Can you tell me more, Josefina?*
Mi hijo, Juan Pablo, tiene un problema. No sé adónde ir para pedir ayuda.	*My son, Juan Pablo, has a problem; I don't know where to go for help.*
¿Qué tipo de problemas está teniendo? ¿Puede decirme más detalles?	*What kinds of problems is he having? Can you tell me more about it?*
Él no está portándose bien en la escuela. La maestra dice que él no presta atención; no está entregando su tarea; y a veces pelea con otros chicos.	*He is acting up in school. The teacher says he is not paying attention; he is not doing his homework; and, sometimes, he gets into fights with other children.*
Ud. debe estar preocupada. Y, ¿dice que todo esto empezó recientemente?	*You must be worried. And you say all of this started happening recently?*
Sí, Marta. En mi país, mi madre me ayudaba.	*Yes, Marta. At home, my mother helped me.*
Las cosas son diferentes aquí. Aquí, las agencias hacen muchas cosas que la familia hace para si misma en tu país.	*Things are different here. Here, agencies do a lot of things that a family does for itself in your country.*
Si, lo sé.	*Yes, I know.*
Pero, volvamos a lo anterior, Josefina. Me dijo que el cambio en el comportamiento de Juan Pablo empezó recientemente. ¿Ha cambiado algo? ¿Piensa que él puede estar preocupado?	*But, let's go back, Josefina. You said the change in Juan Pablo's behavior started recently. Has something changed? Do you think he might be worried?*

Su maestra habló conmigo sobre algo que se llama "A-D-H-D." Ella dijo que a veces los chicos son demasiado agresivos.	*His teacher talked to me about something called "A-D-H-D." I'm not sure what it is; she said boys are sometimes too aggressive.*
Puede ser, pero quizás sea otra cosa.	*It could be, but it may be something else.*
Quizás Juan Pablo esté preocupado por otra cosa. El mes pasado, en la iglesia, el Padre Alex nos pidió que orara por otra familia porque el papá había sido mandado de vuelta a México. Sus papeles eran "malos." Creo que Juan Pablo está preocupado por su papá.	*Maybe Juan Pablo is worried about something else. Last month, in church, Father Alex asked us to pray for another family whose dad had been sent back to Mexico. His papers were "bad." I think Juan Pablo is worried about his dad.*
Juan Pablo podría estar preocupado.	*Juan Pablo might be worried.*
Marta, nunca le hemos dicho a Juan Pablo la razón que salimos de El Salvador. Era demasiado difícil. Queríamos poner los recuerdos de la guerra atrás. Por eso, él no se da cuenta que tenemos "papeles buenos." Estamos aquí legalmente.	*Marta, we've never told Juan Pablo the reason we left El Salvador. It was just too hard. We wanted to put memories of the war behind us. So, Juan Pablo does not realize that we have "good papers." We are here legally.*
Quizás sea tiempo de decirle a Juan Pablo la historia de su inmigración. Te acompañaré a la escuela para hablar con la maestra.	*Maybe it is time to tell Juan Pablo your migration story. I'll go with you to his school to talk with the teacher.*
Gracias, Marta.	*Thanks, Marta.*
Dios la bendiga, Josefina.	*God bless you, Josefina.*

5. Durante la semana que viene
During the coming week

Escriba una carta para hacerle acordar de las actividades que usted quiere hacer para seguir aprendiendo el español. Elija por lo menos tres cosas; anote cuántas veces por semana por cuánto tiempo intenta hacer cada una. Use el modelo del apéndice, "Carta a mí mismo," si quiere.

Ponga la carta en un sobre y manténgala en un lugar seguro. Marque en el calendario un mes después de hoy. En esa fecha, lea la carta y vea si usted ha logrado sus metas. Seleccione nuevos objetivos para el próximo mes. Escríbase una nota de felicitaciones; dése una engomada brillante—o, si usted no ha tenido mucho éxito, elija objetivos más limitados que pueda cumplir.

Write a letter to remind yourself of activities that you want to do to continue learning in Spanish. Choose at least three things; note how many times a week and for how long you intend to do each. Use the model in the appendix, "Carta a mí mismo," if you wish.

Put the letter in an envelope and keep it in a safe place. Mark a date a month from now on your calendar. On that date, read the letter and see if you met your goals. Select new objectives for next month. Write yourself a congratulatory note; give yourself a bright sticker—or, if you have not been too successful, choose more limited objectives that you can complete.

6. Actividades para divertirse
Activities for fun

Hay varios libros disponibles que hablan acerca de las transiciones migratorias; abajo hay algunos títulos y descripciones breves. Algunos son acerca de los latinos; otros están enfocados en otros grupos de inmigrantes en los EE.UU. Algunos están escritos en inglés; otros en español e inglés. Leer es una buena manera de expandir su vocabulario y su conocimiento de la vida de los inmigrantes latinos. ¡Disfrútelos! ¡Buena suerte!

Several books are currently available that address immigration transitions; below are some titles and short descriptions. Some are about Latinos; others focus on other groups who are immigrants to the United States. Some are written in English; others are in Spanish and English. Reading is a good way of stretching your vocabulary and your knowledge of Latino immigrant life. Enjoy! Good luck!

Picture Books
A Movie in My Pillow / Una película en mi almohada by Jorge Argueta (Children's Book Press, 2001). Young Jorge moves to San Francisco from his beloved El Salvador, carrying with him sights and sounds of his rural home. He also carries the memories of loved ones left behind. In English and Spanish.

My Diary from Here to There / Mi diario de aquí hasta allá by Amada Irma Pérez (Children's Book Press, 2002). Amada overhears her mamá and papá whispering about leaving their little house in Juárez, Mexico, and moving to the United States. She is afraid to leave. She worries she won't be able to learn English. Through her family and her diary, Amada learns about her own strength and finds a new home. In English and Spanish.

Young Readers: Fiction
Any Small Goodness by Tony Johnston (Scholastic, 2001). Moving from Mexico to Los Angeles with a little English in his pocket, eleven-year-old Arturo Rodríguez struggles to make sense of his world. Arturo's journey includes reclaiming his heritage, valuing his teachers and mentors, and rescuing the family cat. Still, he must search for the good in life. In English; grades 4–8.

The Gold-Threaded Dress by Carolyn Marsden (Candlewick Press, 2002). In America, Oy's teacher renames her "Olivia." Having just come from Thailand, Oy is unaccustomed to many behaviors she encounters in school, from being left out of games to being teased. Will Oy betray her family to fit in? In English; grades 3–5.

Young Adult: Nonfiction

Breaking Though: Sequel to the Circuit by Francisco Jiménez (Houghton Mifflin, 2001). These stories tell of the struggles of the Jiménez family to cope with separation, poverty, prejudice, and hope. Each episode reveals the tenacity forged by dedication to a goal and reveals how simple gifts from generous people make big differences in the lives of children and adults. In English; grades 7–12.

Journey of the Sparrow by Fran Leeper Buss and Daisy Cubias (Lodestar, 1991). Maria, a sixteen-year-old Salvadoran refugee, cares for her siblings during their difficult journey to Chicago. Together, they start a new life with help from their community. In English; grades 7–12.

Adult: Immigration and Health

From Generation to Generation: The Health and Well-being of Children in Immigrant Families edited by Donald J. Hernandez and Evan Charney (National Academy Press, 1998). This review focuses on policy issues—including acculturation, conditions in receiving communities, parental education and employment, fluency in English, and delivery of health and social services—that shape the lives of immigrant children and youth growing up in the United States.

The Spirit Catches You and You Fall Down by Anne Fadiman (Noonday Press, 1997). This compelling documentary, though not focused on Latinos, does explore the relationships between Lia, a Hmong child, her parents, and her American doctors. Lia Lee, diagnosed with severe epilepsy, was born in the United States rather than in the highlands of northwest Laos, where her parents and twelve brothers and sisters were born. The mutual lack of cultural understanding leads to a clash of two cultures and tragic results.

7. En la comunidad
In the community

⌧ Algunos de los días de fiesta de América Latina también se celebran en América del Norte. Pero los ritos, las creencias, y las comidas pueden ser diferentes. Y éstos también pueden variar de país a país. Abajo se da una descripción corta de estas festividades. Busque en su biblioteca local o en la Red otras descripciones sobre estas fiestas. La próxima vez que tenga la oportunidad, pregúntele a un amigo latino o a un paciente acerca de las festividades que celebran en su país.

☺ *Some holidays that are celebrated in Latin America are also celebrated in North America. But the rituals, the beliefs, and the foods may be different. These may also vary from country to country. Short descriptions of several holidays are given below. Look in your local library or on the Web for more extensive descriptions of typical practices. The next time you have the opportunity, ask a Latino patient or friend how she and her family celebrate a particular holiday in their country.*

Día de los muertos—*On November 1, this festival honors the spirits of the dead. In North America, on October 31, many people celebrate Halloween, a word meaning "hallowed evening." In Spanish-speaking countries, families visit the cemetery on November 1. They dress in holiday clothing and bring food and flowers to the graves of their loved ones.*

La Fiesta de la Virgen de Guadalupe—*This feast is celebrated on December 12. The feast commemorates the appearance of a "Lady from Heaven" to a poor Indian man on a hill northwest of Mexico City in 1531. She identified herself as the Mother of the True God, told him to have the bishop build a temple on the site, and left an image of herself imprinted miraculously on his* tilma, *a piece of poor quality cloth made from cactus. The cloth, which should have worn out within twenty years, is still in perfect condition today! The Virgin's message is one of love and compassion; her promise is to help and protect all mankind. La Fiesta de la Virgen de Guadalupe is celebrated by many Mexican Catholics with a parade that begins in the church sanctuary and spills out onto the plaza. Many Mexican immigrants reenact this traditional celebration in their churches in the United States.*

Navidad—*In Mexico, the Christmas season begins on the sixteenth of December with the celebration of Las Posadas. The people of the town walk from home to home, reenacting the journey of Mary and Joseph to Bethlehem and their search for a place for their baby to be born.*

Día de los Reyes Magos—*January 6 is celebrated as the day that the three kings, Melchor, Baltazar, y Gaspar, arrived to pay homage to Christ. The date marks the end of the Christmas season.*

Carnaval—*Carnaval is a time of celebration that comes just before the start of Lent, a period of fasting and sorrow for Christians. The word comes from Latin and means "good-bye to meat." The day is also called "Fat Tuesday" or "Shrove Tuesday." Two of the most famous carnavals are in the Americas. One is in Rio de Janeiro, Brazil; the other is Mardi Gras in New Orleans! But other Latin American and Caribbean countries, including Ecuador, Peru, and Colombia also celebrate carnaval with their own traditional customs.*

Día de la Independencia—*Most Latin American countries—north, south, and central—celebrate a national independence day. Here are the dates for some countries' celebrations.*

Argentina	May 25, 1810	Guatemala	September 15, 1821
Bolivia	August 6, 1825	Honduras	September 15, 1821
Chile	September 18, 1810	Nicaragua	September 15, 1821
Colombia	July 20, 1810	Mexico	September 16, 1810
Dominican Republic	February 27, 1844	Paraguay	May 15, 1811
Ecuador	August 10, 1809	Peru	July 28, 1821
El Salvador	September 15, 1821	Uruguay	August 25, 1825

8. Diálogo: Apoyo social de la comunidad
Dialogue: Social support in the community

Español	English
◆ Hola, Josefina. ¿Cómo estás? ▶ Muy bien, Ana.	◆ *Hi Josefina. How are you?* ▶ *Very well, Ana.*
◆ Te llamé ayer, pero no contestaste el teléfono. ¿Dónde estabas? ▶ Estuve en el centro latino. Tuvimos una reunión del club de mujeres.	◆ *I called you yesterday, but you did not answer the phone. Where were you?* ▶ *I was at the Latino center. We had a "club de mujeres" meeting.*
◆ ¿Qué es el club de mujeres? ▶ Es un grupo de mujeres. Nos reunimos cada semana y charlamos sobre nuestras dificultades de vivir en este país. A veces nos juntamos a cocinar.	◆ *What is the club de mujeres?* ▶ *It is a women's group. We get together each week and we chat about the challenges of living in this country. Sometimes, we even cook together.*
◆ Parece interesante. ¿Cómo te enteraste sobre una actividad así? ▶ Por medio de una americana que conocí en la clase de natación de Juanito.	◆ *Sounds good. How did you learn about such an activity?* ▶ *Through an American lady that I met at Juanito's swimming lesson.*
◆ ¿Quién es ella? ▶ Ella es la mamá de un buen amigo de mi hijo Juanito. También es la directora del centro latino.	◆ *Who is she?* ▶ *She is the mother of a good friend of my son Juanito. She is also the director of the Latino center.*
◆ Y, ¿cuándo se junta el club de mujeres otra vez? ▶ La próxima semana. ¿Quieres ir conmigo?	◆ *And when does the club de mujeres meet again?* ▶ *Next week. Do you want to go with me?*
◆ ¡Me encantaría! ▶ Bueno, te llamaré el día antes para recordarte.	◆ *I would love to!* ▶ *Then I will call you the day before the meeting to remind you.*

Appendixes

The Basics of Spanish Pronunciation and Accentuation[1]

Selected Consonants

Letter	Approximate sound
h	Always silent (e.g., historia, hospital, exhalar)
j	Like *h* in English "hat" (e.g., joven, jaula, fijar)
ll	In some parts of Spain and Spanish America, like the English *y* in "yet"; generally in Castilian Spanish, like the *lli* in English "million" (e.g., castillo, silla)
ñ	Like *ni* in English "onion" or *ny* in English "canyon" (e.g., niño, pañal)
rr	Strongly trilled (e.g., carro, arriba)
q	Like *k* in English "kite" (e.g., qué, quedar, aquel, aquí)

Vowels

Letter	Approximate sound
a	Like *a* in English "far," "father" (e.g., casa, mano)
e	When stressed, like *a* in English "pay" (e.g., dedo, cerca)
	When unstressed, it has a shorter sound like in English "bet," "net" (e.g., estado, decidir)
i	Like *i* in English "machine" or *ee* in "feet" (e.g., fin, salí)
o	Like *o* in English "obey" (e.g., sol, poner)
u	Like *u* in English "rule" or *oo* in "boot" (e.g., atún, luna)
	It is silent in "gue" and "gui" (e.g., guerra, guisado)
	It is also silent in "que" and "qui" (e.g., querer, quinto)
y	When used as a vowel, it sounds like the Spanish *i* (e.g., y, rey)

Accentuation

- Words that end in a consonant (except *n* or *s*) stress the last syllable: pared, capaz, comer.
- Words that end in a vowel or in *n* or *s* stress the next to the last syllable: casa, pasan, libros, chocolate.
- Words that have an accent mark stress the syllable where the accent mark is placed: café, árbol, máximo.

---

1. Excerpted and adapted from Spanish–English section of the *VOX Compact Spanish and English Dictionary*, 2nd ed., pp. vii–ix.

Answer Key for Mental Health Pasos

Paso Uno

Práctica A
1. Carolina es una trabajadora de salud mental.
2. Ellas están en casa de María Guadalupe.
3. En la mesa están los libros, el florero, el salero, el microondas, y las servilletas.
4. María Guadalupe es de Guatemala.
5. La mujer latina está frustrada al comienzo, pero está mejor ahora.

Práctica B
1. María Guadalupe está preocupada.
2. Luisa tiene calor.
3. Luisa tiene celos de su hermana.
4. Miguel tiene fiebre.
5. Pedro es hondureño.
6. Roberto es médico.
7. Ella tiene hambre.
8. El niño está resfriado.
9. Ana está en la clínica.
10. Los hombres tienen la culpa.

Prácticas C, D, E, F—no key

Actividades para divertirse

Paso Dos

Práctica A—no key

Práctica B

me
se
me
te
se
nos
se
se

Prácticas C, D, E, F, G, H—no key

Actividades para divertirse

P	S	I	H	S	A	B	S	L	A	B	Z	E
R	C	D	E	P	P	I	T	R	I	S	T	E
E	A	N	I	E	O	E	N	O	J	A	D	O
O	N	T	E	G	N	E	N	D	Q	L	A	C
C	S	M	I	R	E	I	E	A	E	O	L	O
U	A	E	A	M	R	A	R	J	H	T	G	M
P	D	G	R	B	I	D	V	O	C	N	O	P
A	O	O	O	O	N	D	I	N	B	E	P	A
D	V	S	R	D	E	S	O	E	B	I	Q	D
A	N	R	I	T	N	E	S	E	N	T	I	R
B	M	A	D	R	I	N	A	E	S	E	H	E
D	E	P	R	I	M	I	D	O	A	M	O	N

Busque estas palabras y traduzca en inglés:
Look for the following words and then translate them into English:

Cansado—*tired*   Deprimido—*depressed*   Enojado—*angry*
Compadre—*godfather* Madrina—*godmother*   Nerviosa—*nervous*
Preocupada—*worried* Poner—*to put*   Tímido—*shy*
Triste—*sad*   Sentir—*to feel*   Sobrino—*nephew*

Paso Tres

Práctica A

Español	English
Ellos ayudaron	*We feared*
Él fue	*We helped*
Nosotros fuimos	*You felt (plural)*
Yo sentí	*I was*
Tú temiste	*She went*
Ella puso	*You felt*

Práctica B

visité

tuvo

hablé

sintió

Prácticas C, D, E, F, G, H—no key

Paso Cuatro

Práctica A

bebían

usaba

tomaba

dormían

miraban

sentía

comía

estaba

Práctica B

siento

sentía

tomaba

limpiaron

cocinaron

tiene

Práctica C

Preterit	Imperfect
bebieron	bebían
tomó	tomaba
puse	ponían
estuviste	estaba
fumaron	fumabas
juzgaste	juzgaban

Prácticas D, E, F, G, H, I, J—no key

Práctica K

1. fumó
2. uso
3. tuvo
4. tomábamos
5. comparte
6. vivía

Paso Cinco

Práctica A

traducir	armonía
apenas	juntos
respeto	celebrar
severo	trabajar
cumpleaños	rebelde

Práctica B

conoció
conocer
hablaron
mostraba
estaba
quería
tienen
supo
sabían
iban
conocer
contestaron

Prácticas C, D, E, F, G, H—no key

Paso Seis

Práctica A

	Translation
1. gusta	*I like to go to church.*
2. gusta	*She likes to study English.*
3. gusta	*José does not like to drink water.*
4. gustan	*The children like the toys.*
5. gusta	*Rosa likes to eat cakes.*
6. gustan	*Friends like to be together.*

Práctica B—no key

Práctica C

A	I	S	L	A	D	O	E				
			A		C	U	L	T	U	R	A
	E	S	P	O	S	O	E		R		T
L	S	U	E	L	T	O	M		E		R
U	T		L				E		Z	E	Á
C	A		V	E	C	I	N	D	A	D	S
H	R						T		R	A	
A	P	O	Y	O			O			D	
R		A	U	T	O	E	S	T	I	M	A
		S	U	P	E	R	A	R			

Prácticas D, E, F, G—no key

Durante la semana que viene

Una carta a mí mismo
A letter to myself

(Please write a short note to yourself describing three things that you plan to do next month to improve your Spanish language skills. Include reference to rewards and incentives that you know will work for you!)

Dear _____ ,

Good luck,

Introducción al Juego "Memoria"
Introduction to the Memory Game

The template that follows provides a set of examples. We have used them to play a Spanish version of "Memory" or "Concentration," a child's game that nearly everyone has played—and remembers.

To make a set of these cards yourself, use the English and Spanish phrases suggested, or make up cards with similar phrases that you want to practice (a blank template is provided). We usually work with a set of about ten to twenty sentences for each language, that is, twenty to forty cards per topic or theme. Print or copy the English phrases onto card stock of one color and the Spanish phrases onto a similar paper in another color. The rectangular graphic design pictured above may be copied onto the backs of both sets of cards.

To play this version of the game, place all cards face down on the table. The first player picks up two cards. The first card must be a card that has a Spanish language phrase. Then, before picking up a second card, the player or teammates must say the phrase in Spanish. Then the same player picks up a card that has an English phrase on it. If the Spanish card is a match to the English card, then the player gets a second turn—but a player may match only two pairs per turn! Then play passes to the second player and the same steps are repeated.

Often, a group will follow the rules as we've described them. Other times, however, we find an enthusiastically engaged group that has "rewritten" the rules—to adapt the challenge to their learning needs. In all cases, we find that the familiarity of playing an old childhood game transformed makes for a fun, cheerful, and competitive atmosphere— where repetition of common phrases takes the work out of learning Spanish. "Let's do this again" is a frequent refrain!

La Consejera	La Esposa	La Inyección
El Psiquiatra	El Abuelo	La Preocupación
La Enfermera	La Hermana	Dolor de Cabeza

Counselor	Psychiatrist	Nurse
Wife	Grandfather	Sister
Injection	Worry	Headache

Un Borracho	Sofocar	La Iglesia
El Examen de Aliento	Empullarse	La Mano
Los Calmantes	La Marijuana	La Cabeza

Drunkard	To choke	Church
Breathalyzer Test	To shoot up	Hand
Sedatives	Marijuana	Head

¿Cómo está usted?

El Centro de Salud Comunitario

Ayudar

Buenos días. Yo soy la enfermera.

¿Qué cosas hace para sentirse mejor?

Siéntese por favor.

¿Ha cambiado su apetito?

¿Sabe el nombre de esta medicina?

Usted parece estar cansada también. ¿Duerme bien?

How are you?	Good morning. I am the nurse.
Community Health Center	What things do you do to make yourself feel better?
To help	Sit down, please.

Has your appetite changed?

Do you know the name of this medicine?

You also seem to be tired. Do you sleep well?

¿Le ha pasado o ha visto un evento traumático?

¿Usó otras sustancias como la marijuana u otras drogas?

Debe ser muy difícil trasladarse a un lugar nuevo.

Le voy a recetar un medicamento.

¿Por cuánto tiempo tomaba?

Si usted quiere, yo me puedo ver con toda la familia un día y hablar con ellos.

¿Qué lo trae aquí?

¿Tomó bebidas alcohólicas con su amigo?

Y, ¿por qué?

What brings
you here?

I will prescribe
a medication.

Have you
experienced or seen
a traumatic event?

Did you drink
alcoholic beverages
with your friend?

How long were
you drinking?

Did you use any
other substance,
like marijuana
or other drugs?

And why?

If you want,
I could meet with the
whole family one
day and talk to them.

It must be difficult
to move to
a new place.

About the Authors

DEBORAH BENDER, PHD, MPH is a professor in the School of Public Health at the University of North Carolina and codirector of Pasos, the Language and Culture Learning Initiative. Her professional training is in medical anthropology and public health policy; she studied Spanish as an undergraduate. She has worked extensively in the Andean countries of South America and with immigrant Latina populations in North Carolina.

In Bolivia, she has collaborated with the University of San Simon in Cochabamba since 1986. Her research and consultations have focused on the effect of migration status on use of health services; changes in breastfeeding and child-spacing practices as a result of urbanization; and improving utilization of health services for prenatal care and birth through community-based interventions.

In the United States, Deborah and co-investigators have trained Latina women as community photographers to elicit perceptions of barriers to preventive health-service use that may not be revealed through direct questioning. Currently, she is training health professionals in North Carolina in communicative Spanish and related cultural competencies so as to improve the quality of care offered to the immigrant Latino population.

CHRISTINA HARLAN, BSN, MA, is a research instructor in the School of Public Health at the University of North Carolina. She earned a BSN from American University in Washington, D.C., and an MA in medical anthropology from The New School for Social Research in New York City. Chris worked for many years with migrant and seasonal farm workers training natural leaders as lay health advisors. These programs were offered in Spanish, Haitian Creole, and English so as to be responsive to the diversity within the farm worker population in North Carolina.

She serves as codirector, with Deborah Bender, of Pasos, the Language and Culture Learning Initiative, sponsored by the North Carolina AHEC, which provides training to health professionals in North Carolina. She is currently teaching Culturally Competent Health Organizations in the School of Public Health. Content is based on the US Office of Minority Health's National Standards for Culturally and Linguistically Appropriate Services in Health (CLAS). Chris has worked as a community/public health nurse in Latin America, the Caribbean, as well as in multiethnic, multilingual rural, and urban communities in the United States. She speaks Spanish and some Haitian Creole.

LINDA KO, MS, MPH, is a doctoral student in the Department of Health Behavior and Health Education in the School of Public Health at the University of North Carolina at Chapel Hill. She has an MS from the University of Texas at El Paso and an MPH from Boston University. She speaks Korean, Spanish, and English fluently.

Linda worked as an English–Spanish, Korean–Spanish, and Korean–English interpreter in El Paso, Texas. She has also worked as a project manager in breast and cervical cancer studies promoting screening practices in minority women, including Latina women in Boston. In North Carolina, she has also assisted in interviewing Latinos as part of an effort to develop a Spanish health literacy tool. Currently, her research focuses on the quality of minority patients' communication with their health care providers.

IRWIN STERN, PHD, earned his doctorate in Luso-Brazilian language and literature with a minor in Spanish from the City University of New York. He has taught both Portuguese and Spanish. He has multiple scholarly publications in the areas of Portuguese and Brazilian and Spanish literatures. In 1978 he facilitated the development of a Medical Spanish program at Columbia University's College of Physicians and Surgeons; he directed this program from 1987 to 1997. He has published *Triage Spanish: Conversational Spanish for Health Professionals* and has taught workshops and immersion courses in medical Spanish with the North Carolina Immigrant Health Initiative. He currently teaches at North Carolina State University.

CPSIA information can be obtained
at www.ICGtesting.com
Printed in the USA
LVHW010551270122
709553LV00005B/501